The Peer Family in North America
V. 1: Jacob & Anne Peer, Immigrants from New Jersey to Upper Canada in 1796

A study of the first two generations
Revised Edition

by Lorine McGinnis Schulze

ISBN: 978-1-987938-01-2

Cover Image Credit: Library and Archives Canada, Acc. No. 1990-586-3
Maps by Brian L. Massey

Introduction

My grandmother Olive McGinnis was a Peer by birth. My website Olive Tree Genealogy is named in her honour. My father, one of her six sons, knew very little of his ancestry. He often spoke about wanting to know more and his early death at age 47 prompted me to find the answers he had so long sought.

Researching the Peer families in North America has been a labour of love. In the last 30 years I have accumulated a great deal of information and source documents. There are several ways I could have tackled the task of compiling these findings, and the findings that other descendants have kindly shared.

Publishing the findings as one book proved to be impossible. The size of it would have been overwhelming. The cost would have been prohibitive. Thus I decided to split what would have been a 1000 pages or more sized book into smaller separate volumes. Splitting the book into separate volumes has the added benefit of allowing descendants to purchase their direct family line at a greatly reduced cost rather than pay for one huge book with information that might not be of interest to them.

Volume 1 is an overview of Jacob, his wife Anne and their known children. All descendants will need Volume 1, as it provides data and documentation for Jacob and Anne.

Each of Jacob and Anne's known or probable children are listed in Volume 1, along with their spouses, birth years and locations and death years and locations when known. Volumes 1 to 7 will contain source documents, details, and a genealogy report up of descendants for each of Jacob and Anne's children.

John Peer & his wife the widow of Thomas Millard are found in this Volume. The list of volumes for the remainder of Jacob and Anne's children is below.

- **Levi Peer & his wife Elizabeth Marical** (settled in Illinois & Ontario). Includes notes, documents, photographs and a genealogy report
- **Edward Peer & his two wives Anna and Sarah** (settled in Pennsylvania & Ontario) Includes notes, documents, photographs and a genealogy report
- **Philip Peer & his two wives Ester Dunn and Susan Griniaus** (settled mainly in Ontario) Includes notes, documents, photographs and a genealogy report
- **Jacob Peer Jr. & his wife Lucy Powers** (settled in Michigan & Ontario) Includes notes, documents, photographs and a genealogy report
- **Stephen Peer & his wife Lydia Skinner** (settled in New York & Ontario) Includes notes, documents, photographs and a genealogy report
- **Phoebe Peer & her husband Daniel McQueen** (settled mainly in Ontario)
- **Marcy Peer & her husband Harcor Lyons** (settled in Michigan & Ontario)

I reluctantly made the decision to follow only the male lineage, that is, to follow the Peer surname only. I have included documentation for women, their spouses and children in hopes this will help those descended from a female Peer to find their placement in the line. I can also be contacted privately for more information on females in the Peer family.

Another choice I made after much deliberation was to focus my research on the early generations from 1780 to 1850. This means that these earlier generations will often have more documentation in the form of land records, birth records, marriage records, death records, census and other miscellaneous documents, than the later generations. From 1850 to 1900 I focused mainly on census records to compile family groups. I have made an effort to include vital statistic records (births, marriages and deaths) where possible, but please remember that there may very well be many more records available for your direct ancestor.

Volume I is the story of Jacob and Anne Peer. Documents are provided as well as source notations for each. A list of their known children and spouses is also given but for details and documents on their children, descendants will also need the next volume which pertains to their specific ancestor.

I hope that the research I am sharing in the Volumes on the Peer Family is of interest and help to you in your genealogy but please remember that this book is copyright, as are all published books. It may not be republished in whole or in part without my written consent.

Table of Contents

Peer Origins 1

Jacob Peer & His Wife Anne 3

Jacob & Anne's Children 9

Jacob Peer Timeline 12

Peer Family of New Amsterdam 14

John Peer & His Wife, the Widow of Thomas Millard 33

Maps 42

Documents for Jacob Peer 45

Documents for John Peer 58

Grandchildren of Jacob & Anna Peer 70

Debunking the Myths 75

Other Ontario Peer Families: Peter Peer & Mary Graham 77

Other Ontario Peer Families: Richard Peer & Elizabeth Shouldice 82

Other Ontario Peer Families: Andrew Peer & Helena Williamson 85

Other Ontario Peer Families: Andrew Peer & Elizabeth 87

DNA Research 88

Endnotes 89

Peer Origins

Little is known of the origins of Jacob Peer who came from New Jersey to Upper Canada (present day Ontario) in 1796. From census records of later generations we know that the family was either Dutch or German in origin. How or when the family arrived in North America remains a mystery, for Jacob has not been found before 1784 at which time he was almost certainly in his 50s.

The Peer surname has been found recorded in a variety of ways – Peer, Pear, Pierre, Pier, Pyer are but a few. This adds to confusion among researchers and the original spelling should be carefully noted when documents are being consulted. Since the name was spelled and mispelled in various ways, one cannot discount a record simply because the name does not look as we expect it to. Instead researchers have to verify the individual through other methods – spousal names, children, locations, and other identifying facts.

It is possible that Jacob Peer was the son of the German immigrant Jacob Peer who took the Oath to the British King when he naturalized in New Jersey on July 8, 1730. It is also possible that Jacob was from the Dutch New Jersey Peer (Pier) family, and that later generations simply confused their Dutch for German heritage, or chose not to mention it due to prejudice. Although there is extensive information on the Dutch Peer family, no firm connection has yet been established to link our Jacob to this line.

The possibility of the Peer family origin as German seems less likely than Dutch origin. Jacob was a known supporter of the British Crown during the American Revolution. If he were not born in the colonies which later became America, he would have no reason to feel loyalty to the British King. The Dutch settled in New Netherland (New York) in the early to late 1600s and later generations felt a great deal of loyalty to the British Monarch.

My personal theory and one I've been working on for many years, is that Jacob Peer is connected to the Dutch Pier family. Their origins in America begin with two brothers Jan Theunisz baptised in Amsterdam Holland in 1631 and Arent Theunisz baptised in the same city in 1637. Jan and Arent and their wives and children sailed from the Netherlands to New Netherland (present day New York) on board St. Jan Baptiste in May 1661.

Arent and his family remained for the most part in New York while Jan's son Teunis Jansen Pier left for New Jersey where he met and married Catarina Tomasse Cadmus.

Many of the New Jersey Pier line spelled their surname Peer. Many disappear from the records and have been difficult to trace down the generations

It is from one of these branches of the Pier family that I suggest our Jacob Peer may be linked but I must stress that this is a theory only and has not been proven. I base my suggestion on pieces of circumstantial evidence but we are a long way from making a solid connection so descendants should not claim this as solid fact.

Perhaps one day the link will be found but currently it is only a working theory.

The article *"Origins of the Pier Family of New York and New Jersey and Their Connection to the Ostrander Family"* by Lorine McGinnis Schulze & Chris Brooks published in the New York Genealogical & Biographical Record July 2000, has been added to aid in understanding the Dutch line from which our Jacob may descend.

Descendants must also be careful not to confuse the several distinctly unique Peer families living in Upper Canada in the early 1800s. One non-related family is the Irish line descended from Andrew Peer from Ireland and his wife Helena, who had a land patent in Beverley Township in 1853. [1] The Irish line of Richard Peer and his wife Elizabeth Shouldice. Richard and Elizabeth lived in Quebec then Ontario by 1881. Another unrelated Peer line is that of Peter Peer and his wife Mary Graham who lived in Leeds County Ontario. Matthew Peer from New York and wife Dorothy House were another family group living in Elgin County Ontario. There were other Peer families but the scope of this Volume does not allow for discussion of them. Descendants should remember that our Peer line from Jacob and Anne is either Dutch or German in origin so others such as Irish or English Peer families can be safely ignored.

Readers should also be cautious using books which rely on pioneer memories or submissions of family genealogies. Although these books are useful for clues to further research, they should never be accepted as accurate without verification. One such example is *The History of the Town of Dundas* published by the Dundas Historical Society. On page 15 we find reference to "... Edward [Peer] and his brothers Jacob, Philip and Andrew ...". Andrew was a Roman Catholic Irishman [2] and is not a member of our Peer family.

As well dozens if not hundreds of online family trees have mistaken other men named Jacob Peer with our immigrant ancestor Jacob. They have erroneously attached him to parents with no proof and no source citations provided (because there are none that prove their claims). In this revised edition I will debunk these erroneous ancestries in hopes of stopping the perpetuation of the errors.

2

Jacob Peer & His Wife Anne

Little is known of Jacob Peer's early life. He first appears in the records of New Jersey in 1774 at which time he was almost certainly a middle-aged man. Unfortunately the early records of New Jersey are sparse, and Jacob's origins cannot be determined with certainty. I suggest that he descends from the Dutch New York Pier line but to date have no proof to substantiate this. His origins are likely German or Dutch as that is the ethnic origin most frequently given by his children and grandchildren in later census records. In the early to mid part of the 19th Century there was prejudice against the Dutch and many individuals of Dutch descent claimed German heritage. This may be the case for our Peer family.

We can estimate Jacob's year of birth as between 1732 and 1742 based on the estimated years of birth of his children. We cannot establish a more precise year of birth as the 1790 New Jersey census is missing which would provide ages. When he settled in Upper Canada it was a wilderness and settlement had only recently begun after the American Revolution ended, thus there are very few records. Those that do exist do not provide ages of individuals.

When Jacob and his family settled in Ontario in 1796 very few records were kept – and between his year of arrival and his death no census records were taken. Birth and marriage records are likewise non-existent, or at least have not been found. Many of the very few early Ontario records are missing and the also complicates research into a very early Ontario family. Many New Jersey records were lost or destroyed during the American Revolution.

The surname of his wife Anne (sometimes referred to as Hannah) is not known and thus her life story is only as complete as what we know of her married years with Jacob. My research has not uncovered her maiden name.

Jacob and his family were living in Newton Township, Sussex County, [3] New Jersey in 1774, [4] and two of his children were married by Squire Franklin Price in Frankford Township, Sussex County in 1782 and 1787 [5]. There are few vital records from 18th century New Jersey and Jacob has not been found prior to this 1774 date. Despite exhaustive research no record of his birth or marriage nor of his children's births has yet been uncovered. That is not surprising since many New Jersey records from this time period were destroyed during the American Revolution.

The 1773 tax rateable list for Newton Township has a total of 324 names, while the 1774 one has only 270. An additional 46 names, Jacob Pear [sic] being one of them, are found on the 1774 tax rateable that were not on the 1773 list, indicating a large migration or population shift in this township just prior to the Revolutionary War. Where was Jacob in 1773? His whereabouts have not yet been found but it is almost certain he was not living in Newton Township that year.

List I in 1774 shows Jacob Pear [sic] of Newton Township Sussex County New Jersey owning 100 acres and 9 cows. [6] Not far from Jacob is Nathaniel Pettit of Newton Township Sussex County. Nathaniel later provided an intriguing but brief affidavit about Jacob and his family during the American Revolution. [7] There is no Jacob Peer of any spelling variation on the September 1773 Newton Township Rateable but Nathaniel and Jonathon Pettit are included in the 1773 list.

Ten years later, in 1784 Jacob and his family were living near Papakatting Creek in Wantage Township. [8] Wantage Township was formed in 1754 from part of Newton Township and Jacob's land was is noted in the land records in 1794 as being "*Lot #2 (6 acres) beside Lot #1 (96 ¾ acres which Jacob had purchased in 1784) and Sharp's Great Tract on Papakating Creek*" From other land records involving Jacob's eldest son Levi Peer, we know that Levi lived near Beemerville, at the head of Papakatting Creek in Wantage Township from at least 1789 to 1800. Almost certainly Jacob and his family lived at the same location. The 1784 purchase of his land places the Peer family in Wantage Township, near Beemerville, as early as 1784.

From Beemerville, it would have been an easy trip downriver on a boat or raft to Frankford, and it is probably the route the family took for events such as baptisms and marriages. Unfortunately almost all the records of this church were lost in a fire; all that survives are a few marriage records, including the marriages of two of Jacob's children in 1782 and 1787. Our knowledge of Jacob's activities for the next few years is limited although we know that his son John Peer left New Jersey for Upper Canada in 1788. [9] John may in fact be the John Peer who deserted from the 3 Battalion, New Jersey Volunteers on 18 February 1788. [10]

Since the 1790 census for New Jersey is missing, we have no way of knowing what Peer families were living there that year. The next available census substitute is the June 1793 tax list which enumerated the head of house only. Here we find the name of Philip Pear (Jacob's son). It seems likely that Jacob, being in his late 50s or 60s, was living with his son Philip at this time and thus his name would not appear independently for taxes.

We find Jacob Peer living in Sussex County New Jersey in 1790.[11] We also find his name on a petition dated 14 Feb 1794, to the "Curt of Comen Please" [Court of Common Pleas] from inhabitants of Sussex County recommending that six surveyors be appointed to Meet at the House of Jacob Pear in Newtown to Relay or lay a Road from the Main Road leading from Newtown to Decker town acrost by Said Pears to a certian Road leading from Thomas Armstrongs to the Bigg Spring. [12]

Jacob Peer was our immigrant ancestor to Ontario. He left Sussex County, New Jersey for Upper Canada (present day Ontario) in 1796, thirteen years after the American Revolution ended. The American Revolution began in 1773 and during this time New Jersey was a hot bed of political and military upheaval. From records found in Ontario we know that Jacob and his family were loyal to the British Crown, and suffered from persecution in New Jersey throughout the war years. His British sympathies had caused great hardship for him during the War, and as former neighbour Nathaniel Pettit described in an affidavit supporing Jacob's petiton for land in Upper Canada.

"[Jacob] suffered greatly both in his person and property in the Late War between Great Britain and America" [13].

In June 1796 Jacob and his son Philip and their families left New Jersey for the wilderness of Upper Canada (Ontario) [14]. Many of these settlers had decided to swear allegiance to the Crown to escape what one settler termed the *"Chaos, Taxes and Anarchy"* of the new republic in the United States [15].

Four of Jacob's sons – Jacob Jr., Edward, John and Philip Peer petitioned for land on the same day in July 1797. [16] Each of the men requested lands as settlers. Each was later granted 200 acres.

A 1792 Proclamation by John Graves Simcoe provided ten conditions for obtaining land in Upper Canada.

Although they did not petition for land until 1797, records reveal that Edward Peer settled in Ancaster in 1786 and John Peer settled in Ancaster in 1788 [17].

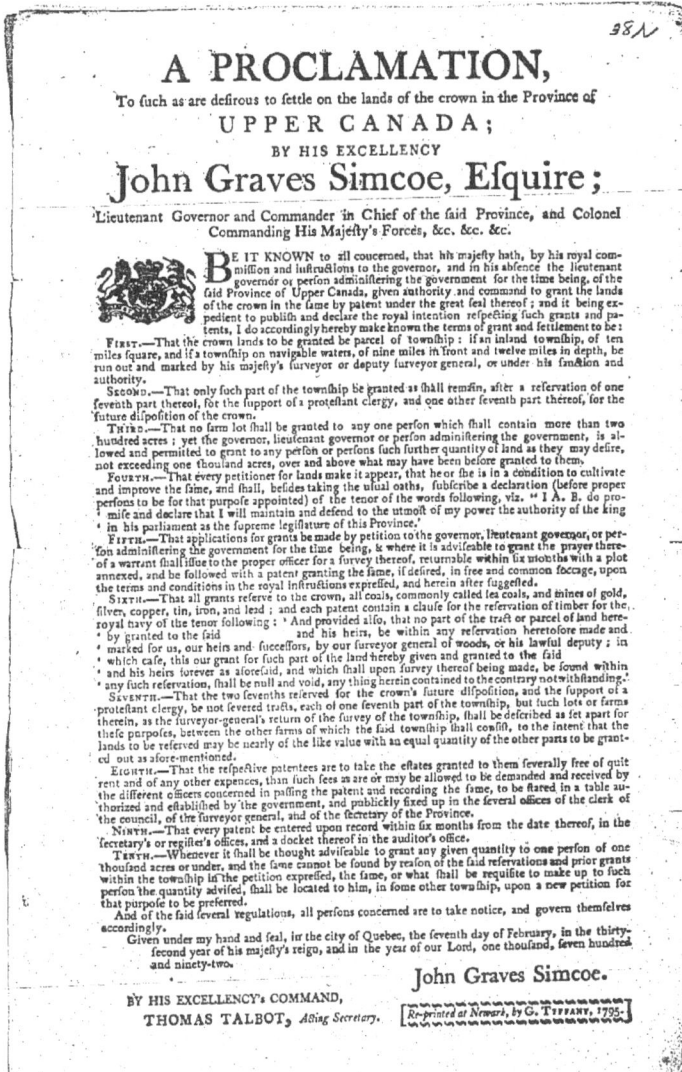

A PROCLAMATION, To such as are desirous to settle on the lands of the crown in the Province of UPPER CANADA; BY HIS EXCELLENCY John Graves Simcoe, Esquire;

Jacob, his wife Anne and at least two of their children settled near Ancaster in Barton Township, Lincoln County Ontario. Their sons Jacob Jr., Philip, John, Stephen and Edward settled nearby. Their two married daughters, Phoebe and Marcy also settled nearby, the only son not yet in Ontario was Levi, who joined them a few years later.

Jacob petitioned for land and provided documentation that he and his family had been sympathizers on the British side during the American Revolution, but his name was never placed on the Loyalist rolls. There were strict requirements for being declared a Loyalist and although it seems obvious to Peer descendants that Jacob Sr should have qualified, he and his sons were not accepted as Loyalists and thus were not able to receive free grants of land given to

Loyalists and their sons and daughters.

During the American Revolution, Loyalists, a large number of whom had joined the British Army, suffered confiscation of property and banishment. After the war ended, many remained in their native or adopted country while others sought refuge in England. At least 35,000 to 40,000 individuals, including disbanded soldiers, sought asylum in Canada. [18]

Immigrants from the 13 British colonies began arriving in Canada in 1774. They were loyal to Great Britain in the American War for Independence and were no longer welcome in the United States.

The largest group influx of United Empire Loyalists to Upper Canada began on the conclusion of the peace by the Treaty of Paris, signed on the 3 September, 1783. In 1784 land along the St. Lawrence River, from Lake St. Francis to Lake Ontario, along the shores of Lake Ontario as far as and including the Bay of Quinté, the town of Niagara, then called Newark, and part of the shores of the Detroit River, were colonized by about 10,000 United Empire Loyalists who received Government aid in the form of rations and land.

Parliament also passed an act authorizing the Crown to settle the amount of the losses Loyalists had sustained by the confiscation of their property, and courts of inquiry were held in in England Halifax, Quebec and Montreal between 1784 and 1788. An Order in Council in November 1789 provided for the settlement of children of the Loyalists.

A British law passed in 1791 divided Canada into Upper and Lower Canada. Upper Canada consisted of what is now present day Ontario; Lower Canada was present day Quebec. In 1800, the population of Upper Canada was about 35,000

When Jacob Peer arrived in Upper Canada it was a wilderness land recently settled by Loyalists fleeing from the United States. Before the end of the American Revolution in 1783 Upper Canada was largely uninhabited.

By 1803 Jacob, a farmer, bought more land in Ancaster. Although Jacob and Anne were in the Niagara area during the War of 1812, they did not file any claims for losses so we have no way of knowing how badly they may have been affected.

From 1812 to 1814 the Niagara region was the battleground of some of the bloodiest battles in Canadian history. On June 18, 1812 the United States declared war against Great Britain (which included Canada). The Americans began with attacks on three fronts - Lake Champlain, the Niagara Frontier, and Detroit.

Early in the morning of October 13, 1812 American troops crossed the Niagara River from Fort Niagara in the hopes of capturing the town of Queenston. Although they outnumbered British troops the Americans were met with fierce resistance and were unable to defeat the British, who were led by General Brock. Brock died during the Battle of Queenston Heights and Jacob Peer's son Stephen was wounded.

On November 28th, 1812, 400 American troops travelled across the Niagara River from Black Creek in an attempt to capture Fort Erie. A second group of Americans set out to destroy Frenchman's Creek bridge, in an effort to delay British reinforcements coming from Chippawa. The British army forced the Americans to retreat back to Black Creek.

On April 27th, 1813 American troops captured and burned the city of York (now Toronto), which was the capital of Upper Canada, and by May 27th they had captured Fort George. Fort George became the headquarters for US forces. Its strategic location was put to good use as they utilized it to invade the rest of Upper Canada. Fort George was eventually reclaimed by the British in December of 1813 and occupied by the British for the remainder of the war.

On June 24th, 1813, British forces stationed at Decew Falls received an advanced warning of an impending US attack when Laura Secord at nearby Beaverdams overheard American troops discussing the impending attack. Knowing that a surprise attack could mean a major blow to the British, she walked 20 miles through wild bush and swamp to warn them.

On December 10, 1813 the Americans who had been held up at Fort George decided to retreat as conditions were worsening due to the harsh winter. On their way back to Fort Niagara they burned the town of Newark, now Niagara-on-the-Lake. At the time the town largely consisted of women and children, and the American troops burned their homes to the ground, leaving them homeless in the middle of a cold December. Every building except one was burned to the ground and many women and children froze to death because they were unable to find shelter from the bitter cold. The British retaliated by capturing Fort Niagara, which had large stores of food, clothing, and weapons. British forces along with their Indian companions burned the surrounding towns of Youngstown, Lewiston, Manchester, and Buffalo, capturing and killing many Americans.

On July 3rd, 1814 6,000 American troops crossed the Niagara River, and took Fort Erie with little resistance from the British. They began advancing north towards Chippawa. As dawn broke on the morning of the 5th of July British forces along with their Indian allies began their advance on the Americans. When they reached Street's Creek the battle began, lasting only half an hour and ending in an American victory. The British sustained heavy losses with 415 men either being killed, wounded or captured, the surviving men forced to retreat under heavy gun fire to Chippawa Creek. Stephen Peer was killed during this battle and his pregnant wife gave birth to their son just one month later.

July 12th, 1814 saw American troops arrive at the village of St. David's. They began looting the village, killing off the livestock and taking whatever they could carry from the homes. American soldiers set the town ablaze, burning over 40 homes and businesses and leaving the villagers homeless.

The battle at Lundy's Lane was fought mainly during the night of July 25th, 1814, involving 5,000 American and 2,200 British, Canadian militia and First Nations fighters. The British lost over 800 men and the Americans over 860. Hundreds of others had been badly wounded or captured by the enemy. The battle ended in a stalemate, with the Americans retreating to nearby Chippawa, then to Fort Erie, burning the small town of Bridgewater along the way.

The Americans moved on to Fort Erie with little resistance. The British arrived at the Fort a few days later ready to fight once again. The British suffered heavy losses in the battle, with over 900 men killed, wounded, or missing. With the onset of heavy rain the British lay low for 13 days before retreating to Chippawa. After several days the Americans returned to the US to defend Buffalo, destroying Fort Erie when they left.

The war saw great losses on both sides it finally concluded when the Treaty of Ghent was signed on Christmas Eve 1814. After the war the Niagara region was in ruins, as many villages and buildings were burned to the ground, and it took nearly a decade to fully restore the area.

Jacob's son Stephen was killed during the War of 1812, and his widow Lydia filed several claims for losses. Another son Jacob Jr also filed for losses sustained in the war. It seems families closer to the Niagara River were more affected by the War. We know from the 1821 sale of their land in Barton Township, that the original deed to Jacob's land was lost or destroyed in the War of 1812.

Early Upper Canada (Ontario) records are scarce, and those that exist are often difficult to find. Thus there are only a few scattered records allowing us to track Jacob until his death circa January 1815. His wife Anne probably died in 1821 as the terms of Jacob's will did not allow his Barton Township farm to be sold until her death, and it was sold April 23, 1821. There are no burial or church records for the death of Jacob or Anne and no trace of their burial location has been found. They may have been buried on their farm as was the custom in those early years in Upper Canada before land began to be set aside for cemeteries. Burial on the family farm usually meant a simple grave marked only by a wooden cross and perhaps a few stones.

Jacob & Anne's Children

We know that Levi, John, Jacob Jr and Philip were sons of Jacob and Anne (as per Jacob's 1810 will and the affidavit of Levi Peer in 1807), and it is almost certain that Edward was another son. They lived near each other, sold each other land, and interacted over dozens of years. Although Jacob did not name Edward in his will, older children were often given their inheritance early, and thus not named in a will. As well, Edward, Levi and Stephen Peer were involved in the administration of John Peer's estate in 1808. I have therefore placed Edward in Jacob's family group as an older son but this is a tentative placement based on circumstantial evidence.

Jacob's will is of great importance in determing the family group. Some children such as Edward may not have been named because they had received their inheritance from their father before he made his will, or, as is the case of his son John, were deceased at the time he wrote his will. Six children named in his will were Jacob Jr., Philip, Levi, Pheobe, Marcy, and Stephen. John, the deceased son, makes seven. We know that Jacob Sr. had at least eight children, possibly nine. Edward fits nicely to make a total of eight.

The land petition of Jacob Peer Jr dated May 1804 state that his "father and mother with eight of their children live near the Head of Lake Ontario....". The question that arises is – did Jacob include himself in this mention of eight children? Or did he mean that there were eight other children besides himself? Although we cannot say with certainty what Jacob Jr. meant, when we take into account Jacob Sr's petition of 1797 wherein he states that he has "a wife and daughter now in Barton..." we reach some interesting albeit puzzling conclusions.

Jacob Sr's two known daughters were Phoebe and Marcy. Both these girls were married well before the 1797 petition. Phoebe had at least 5 children of her own by the time of the 1797 petition, and Marcy had 3. Therefore neither Phoebe nor Marcy were the daughter referred to in 1797. This means Jacob Sr had another daughter before this 1797 date. That conclusion agrees with Jacob Sr. having a total of 9 children and thus Jacob Jr's statement wherein he refers to his father mother and 8 of their children, meaning 8 children besides himself. This means we have the possibility that another daughter, name unknown, was born to Jacob and Anne.

The only child of Jacob Peer for whom we have a fairly exact year of birth is Marcy. A birth date of December 06, 1774 which is very often used by her descendants, is based on her signature on a quilt she embroidered in 1847. However her hand-embroidered quilt the Dundas Museum in Ontario, which she signed as "Marcy Lyons December 6, 1847, 74 years" does not give us her exact birth date, nor does the signed date imply that December 6 was her birthday. In fact it is more likely that December 6th was the date she started or completed the quilt. What we know from the quilt is that she was born circa 1773. Marcy's sister Pheobe's estimated year of birth of 1768 is based on census records. The birth year and location for Jacob Jr. is given in a Pioneer Memory book as 1776 in New Jersey.

We can give a tentative order of children by birth year when we look at all the facts available, such as dates of marriage, dates children were born, dates they purchased land, and so on. We know Levi to be the eldest brother (as per his affidavit dated 13 February 1808) so we can place the children as:

- Levi born circa 1760-1768
- John born circa 1762-1768
- Edward born circa 1764-1768
- Philip born circa 1766
- Phoebe born circa 1768
- Marcy born circa 1773
- Jacob Jr. born circa 1776
- Stephen born circa 1780

Assuming Jacob to be between 20 and 30 at the birth of his first child, this gives him an estimated date of birth of 1732 to 1742.

Children of JACOB PEER and ANNE are:
i. LEVI[3] PEER, b. Abt. 1760, New Jersey?; d. Bef. 1831, Northeast Tp., Erie Co. Pennsylvania; m. ELIZABETH MARICAL, Bet. 1801 - 1802, Ontario?; b. 18 Mar 1783, Schenectady, New York; d. Bet. 1850 - 1860, Wayne City? Hamilton Co. Illinois.
ii. JOHN PEER, b. Abt. 1762, New Jersey; d. 28 Jan 1808, Ancaster Tp. Ontario; m. the WIDOW OF THOMAS MILLARD.
iii. EDWARD PEER, b. 1764, New Jersey; d. 09 Nov 1834, Northeast Tp., Erie Co. Pennsylvania; m. (1) ANNA, Bef. 1792; b. Canada; d. Bet. 1809 - 1812, Ancaster Tp. Ontario; m. (2) SARAH, Bet. 1809 - Jun 1812; b. Abt. 1781; d. 16 Mar 1833, Northeast Tp., Erie Co. Pennsylvania.
iv. PHILIP PEER, b. Abt. 1766, New Jersey?; d. Abt. Oct 1828, Brantford, Brant Co. Ontario; m. (1) ESTHER DUNN, 23 Apr 1792, Frankford Tp. Sussex Co. New Jersey; d. Bef. 1816; m. (2) SUSAN GRINIAUS, Bef. 1816; b. 29 Apr 1800, Berks Co., Reading PA; d. 27 Mar 1871, Erin Tp, Wellington Co. Ontario.
v. PHOEBE PEER, b. Abt. 1768, New Jersey; d. Bef. 1848, Norfolk Co. Ontario; m. DANIEL MCQUEEN, 03 May 1787, Frankford Tp. Sussex Co. NJ; b. 19 Apr 1764, USA; d. 22 Jan 1854, Port Dover, Woodhouse Tp, Norfolk Co. , Ontario.
vi. MARCY PEER, b. 06 Dec 1774, New Jersey?; d. 11 May 1861, West Flamborough Tp. Wentworth Co. Ontario; m. HARCOR LYONS, 18 Oct 1792, Frankford Tp. Sussex Co. New Jersey; b. 09 Mar 1770, Sussex Co. New Jersey; d. 26 Mar 1838, West Flamborough Tp. Halton Co. Ontario.

vii. JACOB PEER, b. Abt. 1776, New Jersey?; d. 14 Feb 1855, Clay, St. Clair Co., Michigan; m. LUCY POWERS; b. Abt. 1778, New Jersey; d. Aft. 1821, Michigan.

viii. STEPHEN PEER, b. Abt. 1780, New Jersey?; d. 05 Jul 1814, Chippewa, Ontario; m. LYDIA SKINNER, 16 Apr 1809, Stamford Ontario?; b. 13 Aug 1785, New York; d. Bef. 1851.

Jacob Peer Timeline

1774: Jacob was living in Newton Township Sussex County New Jersey

1784: On 28 April 1784 Jacob Pier [sic] bought land in New Jersey from Phillip & Mary Riggs. 26 May 1796 Anthony Snover and Jane his wife of Newton to Daniel McElhoran (?) of Newark, Essex County, £800 for 2 lots in Newton Township Lot #1 begins on the original line of Isaac Sharps....being a corner of Hugh Haggerty....96 3/4 acres that was bequeathed by LWT of Isaac Sharp dated 22 March 1770 to Elisabeth Sharp and Joseph Sharp and Grace his wife and they sold to Phillip Riggs (?) on 20 March 1775 and Phillip Riggs and Mary his wife sold to one Jacob Pier on 28 April 1784. [19]

1793 June Tax Lists, Newton, New Jersey - Philip Pear (It is almost certain that Jacob Sr. was with his son Philip at this time.)

1794: Jacob purchased land in Wantage New Jersey on 3 May 1794 from Silas & Mary Hopkins. Lot #2 lays adjacent to Lot #1 and Sharps Great Tract on Pepocotting [sic. This is Pepakating Creek] ....on the division line between Silas Hopkins and Lot #1 ....6 acres which Silas Hopkins and Mary his wife sold to Jacob Pier on 3 May 1794. Signed by Anthony and Jane Snover. Witnesses: David A Ogden. Judge Francis Price. On 29 May 1796 the Grantors have deposition to Judge Francis Price. (The deed does not say how the Snovers got title from Jacob Pier)

1796, June: came to Upper Canada (present day Ontario) from New Jersey with son Philip

1797 July 13: Jacob declared in his Upper Canada land petition that he came to the province [Ontario] in June 1796 and had a wife and daughter in Barton where he owned a farm. He was granted 200 acres on 14 July 1797.[20]

1797 July 14. Orders in Council granted 200 acres Jacob Peer, Barton Tp, Lincoln County District of Niagara, Yeoman. "Brought forward for payment of survey" Entered 21 May 1803 Survey costs 1/7/6. Lot 5 Concession 1 Ancaster

1801: May 1. Joseph Hopkins of Frankford Township New Jersey and Hannah his wife to William Pellet & Obadiah Pellet. This deed mentions Jacob Pier as having recieved the property on 3 May 1794 and sellling the two lots to Anthony Snover. No new information. [21]

1803: July 10. Jacob received the Crown Patent for Concession 1 Lot 5 Ancaster Township 200 acres

1804: Jacob gave the south half of Lot 5 Concession 1 Ancaster Tp to his son Philip

1808: June 21 Jacob Sr. of Barton Tp Concession 8 Lot 20 voted for James Blaney. Jacob of Glanford Township voted for James Blayney

1808: Jacob sold the south half of Lot 5 Concession 1 Ancaster Township to David Almas.

1810: Jacob wrote his will on 29 January 1810

1815: Jacob died. Will probated 21 January 1815

1821: 3 April. Christian Almas declaration re Lot 20, Concession 8 Barton, that the original deed to Jacob Peer Sr, deceased, was lost or destroyed in War of 1812. Executors Jacob Peer Jr and William Rymal now wish to sell this land to Jacob Rymal Jr

Peer Family of New Amsterdam

Origins of the Pier Family in The Netherlands

THE OSTRANDER FAMILY

BY LORINE MCGINNIS SCHULZE AND CHRIS BROOKS*

The authors of this article had not met prior to publication of Mr. Brooks' July 1999 article "Parentage of Pieter Pietersen Ostrander and His Sister Tryntje Pieters" [hereafter "Pietersen Parentage"][1] which established the connection of the Ostrander and Pier families. They had co-incidentally been researching these same families with Mr. Brooks researching the Ostranders while Ms. McGinnis Schulze was researching the Piers. After meeting, the authors decided to combine their research efforts and have since uncovered more information in Amsterdam and other locations in the Netherlands that casts new light on both the Pier and Ostrander families.

Pier Origins. Arent Theunissen and Jan Theunissen arrived in New Netherland 6 August 1661 on the ship *St. Jan Baptiste*.[2] Both men are recorded as being from Amsterdam. Arent Theunissen was described as having a wife and two children ages 7 and 4 years old, and Jan Theunissen had a wife and two children 4 and 1¼ years old.[3] These two men were the ancestors of the Pier families in New York and New Jersey. No definitive genealogy of the family or their origins in Amsterdam has been found. Pier researchers invariably attribute the brothers' baptisms to parents Theunis Jansz (of Deventer, Overijssel) and Jannetie Arents who supposedly married in Amsterdam, but no source citation or date has previously been published.

Since the Amsterdam vital records are readily accessible through the DTB[4] indexes, available both at the Amsterdam Municipal Archives [GAA] and from the Family History Library in Salt Lake City, it was decided to research the origins of the two brothers. The names of the two children on board with Arent Theunissen Pier were previously not known, and only the

* 4931 Elliott Side Road, R.R. 1, Midland ON L4R 4K3 Canada, and 5000 Baltimore, #102, Kansas City, MO 64112-2470. The authors would like to thank Harry Macy for his assistance and editorial suggestions. We also thank Pim Nieuwenhuis of Amstelveen and Monique Pieters of Pumerend for their additional research in Amsterdam and translations of documents on our behalf, and Cor Snabel of Amstelveen for his valuable commentary and translations.

¹ Chris Brooks, "Parentage of Pieter Pietersen Ostrander and His Sister Tryntje Pieters", REC. 130:163-173 [hereafter "Pietersen Parentage"].

² For a list of over 500 ship crossings between Amsterdam and New Amsterdam see Jaap Jacobs, "De Scheepvaart en Handel van de Nederlandse Republiek op Nieuw-Nederland 1609-1675" [The Shipping and Trade from the Dutch Republic to New Netherland 1609-1675], Master's Thesis, University of Leiden, 1989.

³ West India Company Account Book in New York Colonial Mss., vol. 14, Book KK, p. 46, New York State Archives (microfilm copy at NYG&B). This account book is the source for the lists of "Passengers to New Netherland," *Year Book of The Holland Society of New York* 1902:1-37.

⁴ The DTB are the Doop-, Trouw-, en Begraafregisters (Baptism, Marriage, and Burial Registers). For an explanation of the DTB indexes and the records they cover see [Hendrik O. Slok], *Church and Civil Records of Amsterdam, The Netherlands, Before 1811*, Research Paper Series C, No. 25 (Salt Lake City: The Genealogical Society of the Church of Jesus Christ of Latter-day Saints, 1975). The index to baptisms by patronymics, omitted by Slok, is described in Gwen F. Epperson, *New Netherland Roots* (Baltimore: Genealogical Publishing Co., 1994), pp. 38-39. The original records and the indexes are at the Amsterdam Municipal Archives (Gemeente Archief Amsterdam [hereafter GAA]), and are also available on Family History Library microfilm [hereafter FHL].

name of one of the two children of Jan Theunissen Pier was known, Rachel, who married twice in Kingston, New York. Some authors and genealogists have claimed that a mysterious Jan Pier married a Tryntie Pietersen Ostrander, and this Jan Pier was assumed by many researchers to be one of the unknown children on board the *St. Jan Baptiste*. Our research laid this myth to rest, and provided us with the names and baptismal dates of all four children travelling with Jan Theunissen Pier and his brother Arent.

Research in the GAA revealed the marriage intention of Theunis Jansz and Jannetie Arents and the baptisms of several children to them. Among their children were the immigrant Pier brothers, Jan and Arent, substantiating the accepted parentage for these brothers and providing documentation for their dates of baptism.

The marriage intention of Theunis Jansz and Jannetie Arents reads:[5]

Den 14 September 1624

Compareeden als vooren Teunis Jansz *van Deventer, cuyper, out 24 jaeren, vaders en moeders consent bij acte is gebleken, wonende in de Taksteeg ende* Jannetie Arents *van Tuenen, geassisteerd met haar vader Arent Joosten out 22 jaren, wonende op de Singel bij de Tonispoort.*

14 September 1624

Appeared as before, *Teunis Jansz* from Deventer, cooper (vatmaker or barrel maker), 24 years old, father's and mother's permission shown by certificate, living in the Taksteeg, and *Jannetie Arents* from Tuenen, assisted by her father Arent Joosten, 22 years old, living on the Singel near the Tonis gate.

Their marriage occurred in the Oude Kerk (Old Church) on 6 October 1624.[6] The marriage intention revealed that Theunis was born *circa* 1600 probably in Deventer, and Jannetie *circa* 1602 in Tuenen, possibly Tonning which is in present-day Schleswig-Holstein.[7] The record confirmed Jannetie's father as Arent Joosten, also living in Amsterdam in 1624. Written above Arent Joosten's name was the notation that he had been in Amsterdam for 14 years. Thus it is probable that Arent and his family came to Amsterdam *circa* 1610 when Jannetie was a child of about eight.

Although Theunis' parents were not present, he had their permission to marry and thus we know they were alive in 1624. The Deventer records exist for baptisms beginning in 1571 and these were searched for information on Theunis Jansz and his parents. Our findings will be discussed later in this article.

5 Amsterdam Marriage Intentions, 429:242, FHL 0113191.

6 Amsterdam Oude Kerk Marriages, DTB 970, FHL 0113353.

7 At first this record was read as "Tienen" which is in Brabant, Belgium. Because the writing was difficult to decipher, Monique Peters asked Mr. Harmen Snel of the GAA to scrutinize the document on our behalf. Mr. Snel determined that the name in fact was "Tuenen" which could be present-day Tonning, in Schleswig-Holstein. In the 17th century Tonning belonged to Denmark, and it was not far from the island of Nordstrand or the town of Husum in Schleswig-Holstein, places associated with the Ostrander ancestor Pieter Carstensen.

The children of Theunis Jansz and Jannetie Arents were easy to determine as only one couple with these names could be found having children baptized in Amsterdam in this time period. In these baptisms, Theunis Jansz's occupation of *cuyper* confirms that we have the correct man:

Maerijtjen, bap. 7 Sept. 1625, father Tonis Jansz kuyper, mother Jannetjie Arentsz, sp. Aecht Arentz, Hendrickje Dirx.[8]

Willem, bap. 4 July 1627, father Teunis Jansz, mother Jannetje Arents, sp. Trijn Claes.[9]

Jan, bap. 13 Nov. 1629, father Teunis Jansz, kuyper, mother Jannetje Arents, sp. Aecht Arents, Gerrit Jansz.[10]

Jan, bap. 19 Oct. 1631, father Teunis Jansz, kuyper, mother Jannetje Arents, sp. Aecht Arents, Gerrit Jansz.[11]

Maritje, bap. 26 Feb. 1633/34, father Teunis Jansz, mother Jannetje Ernst [*sic*], sp. Jannetje Jacobs.[12]

Arent, bap. 27 Dec. 1637, father Teunis Jansz, kuyper, mother Jannetje Arentse, sp. Bertje Claesdr. Lambertsz.[13]

Arent Joosten. Arent Joosten was named as the father of Jannetie Arents in her marriage intention of 1624. We know he was living in Amsterdam at this time. Our research for those who stood as sponsors at the baptisms of Jannetie Arent's children revealed unexpected information when we found the marriage intention of baptismal sponsor Bertje Claesdr. Lambertsz and Arent Joosten, Jannetie's father![14]

Den 11 Maius 1624

Arend Joosten *van Nieuwveen wedr van Marrij Willems, modderman, woonende aan de Amster [Amstel?] en* Beertie Claes *van Blokszijl weduwe van Dirck Heyndricx, verclaerde over 1 jaer wed. geweest te hebben, won., opt Swaaneveld.*

---

8 Amsterdam Oude Kerk Baptisms, DTB 121:6, FHL 0113132. Aecht Arents, who sponsored the first born child Maerijtjen and both sons named Jan, seemed a good candidate for a sister of Jannetje Arents. Since the DTB Indexes did not show any women named Aecht Arents, we extended our search to include women with the first name Aefje (or variant spellings) but no marriage intention or other records have so far been found.

9 Amsterdam Nieuwe Kerk Baptisms, DTB 40:403, FHL 0113364.

10 Ibid., DTB 41:51, FHL 0113364. It is possible that Gerrit Jansz, who stood as sponsor for the first-born child Maritje and for Jan, was a brother to Theunis Jansz, the father of the Pier brothers who came to New Netherland. With this in mind we searched the marriage records of Amsterdam and found two marriages for a Gerrit Jansz from Deventer. He married (as the widower of Annetjen Hendrixdr) with intention dated 9 Apr. 1611, Trijn Jansdr from Goesfeld, age 35 (Marriage Intentions, 415:38, FHL 0113187). As the widower of Trijn Jansdr he married, with intention dated 20 June 1626, Aechten Pieters from Amsterdam, age 38 (Marriage Intentions, 431:260, FHL 0113192). Although neither of Gerrit's marriage intentions provide us with his age, we know that at his marriage as a widower in 1611, he was at least 20, and quite likely closer in age to his bride, who was 35. This gives us a year of birth before 1591 and probably closer to 1581. The Deventer Reformed Church records of baptisms have sporadic entries beginning in 1571 and finding Gerrit's baptism is unlikely. No baptism of a brother named Gerrit was found when the Deventer records were checked and other siblings of Theunis Jansz were found (see below). A search for his first marriage record may reveal his relationship, if any, to Theunis Jansz.

11 Amsterdam Oude Kerk Baptisms, DTB 6:319, FHL 0113132.

12 Amsterdam Nieuwe Kerk Baptisms, DTB 41:302, FHL 0113364.

13 Amsterdam Oude Kerk Baptisms, DTB 7:156, FHL 0113133.

14 Amsterdam Marriage Intentions, 429:31, courtesy of Yoram Franzen; also FHL 0113191.

11 May 1624
Arent Joosten from Nieuwveen,[15] widower of Marrij Willems, dredger, residing on the Amster [Amstel?], and *Beertje Claes* from Blokzijl, widow of Dirck Heijndricx who declared that she had been widow for over a year, residing at the Swaaneveld.

Here we learn Arent Joosten's trade — *modderman*, literally "mud man," or dredger. A dredger in Amsterdam was an operator on the dredger-machine used to keep the canals clean and deep enough. The "ship" carried a strange contraption put into motion by a horse, whereby a row of buckets scraped over the bottom and brought the mud to the surface.[16]

The marriage intention reveals the name of Marrij Willems as the probable mother of Jannetie Arents, and grandmother to Jan Theunissen Pier and Arent Theunissen Pier. The fact that Jannetie named her two daughters Maerijtjen/Maritje and a son Willem supports this identification. Arent Joosten's marriage to Marrij Willems is only known from his marriage as Marrij's widower to Baertje Claes in 1624. No record was located in Amsterdam for a marriage of Arent and wife Marrij, nor were baptismal records for any children found. This was not surprising since we expected to find Arent in Tonning (Jannetie's probable place of origin) or in Nieuwveen (Arent's place of origin on his 1624 marriage intention).

Further research provided us with the remarriage of Baertje Claes, as Arent Joosten's widow, with intention dated 20 April 1641:[17]

Den 20 Aprilis 1641
Compareerden als vooren Jan Volckerss *wede van Hilletje Egbertsz, vlotschuytvoerder &* Baertje Claes *weduwe van Arent Joosten. . . .*

20 April 1641
Appeared as before *Jan Volckerss* widower of Hilletje Egbertsz, bargemaster, and *Baertje Claes* widow of Arent Joosten. . . .

There was no mention of the Weeskamer[18] in the margin which meant that there were no underage children whose rights had to be assured. This record provided us with a time frame for the death of Arent. We know he died between 6 October 1624 when he appeared with his daughter Jannetie

---

[15] There are two villages named Nieuwveen located in Zuid Holland and a Nijeveen in Overijssel that are possible places of origin for Arent Joosten. None has church records that go back far enough to permit a search of baptism and marriage records for this family.

[16] Explanation courtesy of Pim Nieuwenhuis.

[17] Amsterdam Marriage Intentions, 455:208, courtesy of Pim Nieuwenhaus and Yoram Franzen; also FHL 0113200.

[18] When a person died leaving behind under-age children, the grave-diggers were obliged to report this to the Weeskamer, or Orphan Court. The Weeskamer maintained a burial book for each church, where information regarding the deceased person was entered, with space left for additional information at a later date. This additional information included the Weeskamer's notations, made when the widowed spouse was about to remarry. When permission to remarry was sought, the Weeskamer asked for details on the deceased spouse's date and place of death and burial, and for a declaration as to the rights of any underage children. The Weeskamer entered the information in the margin of the church books which were kept in chronological order by date of death. Thus in order to find a Weeskamer record, the date and place of burial of the deceased must be known.

at her marriage intention, and 20 April 1641 when his widow Baertje Claes remarried.

A search of the Amsterdam notarial indexes was conducted but no record was found of Arent Joosten.[19] Two death records were found for an Arent/Arien Joosten in Amsterdam. One was for a burial 24 September 1636 in Karthuisers Kerkhoff (along with 41 other people buried that day), but the full entry was not found.[20] The second was for an Arent Joosten buried in the Zuiderkerk: *Begravaen den 19 ditto [November 1630] Arent Joosten Lotten A no 8*.[21]

Pier in Deventer. Our search now turned to Deventer where we hoped to find the baptism of Theunis Jansz who was born *circa* 1600 according to his marriage intention of 6 October 1624. Deventer used to be a very important Hanseatic town (*Hanzestad*), a trade link between the Rhine and the Baltic Sea (*Oostzee*). In the 12th century its walls were built and in the 13th and 14th century it became a thriving and rich trading center. During the rebellion against Spain and especially during the occupation by the Germans under Count van Rennenberg in 1578, the rich churches and convents were plundered, the citizens robbed of all their belongings, and trade and prosperity severely damaged; the city never fully recovered.[22] The available Deventer records include the *Poerterboeken* (Citizens' or Freemen's Registers) from 1595, and baptisms which begin in 1571.[23] Theunis' baptism was found in 1603, to parents Jan Pier and Aeltijen Willems van Essen. Other children were found for this couple under variations of the surname: Pijr/Pier/Pijer/Peer. This suggests that the Pier name was an established surname in the Netherlands, and provides a reason for the family to begin using it again in New York.[24]

Jan Pijr [Pier/Pijer/Peer] and Aeltijen Willems van Essen had the following children, all baptized at Deventer, Overijssel:[25]

Toeniss, bap. 1 May 1603, sp. Cornelis kock, Willem van Essen, Geertijen nich [nien?] Voss.
Jan, bap. 23 Sept. 1604, sp. Gerlich Fijsscher, Jan Ijnden Fos [Vos], Kornelis Kockij maecht.

[19] Most of the notarial documents in the GAA have not been indexed and searching all the records would be a monumental task, so finding nothing in the current indexes does not preclude finding records in the future.
[20] Amsterdam Karthuizers Kerkhoff Burials, DTB 1148:99, FHL 0114698.
[21] Amsterdam Zuiderkerk Burials, DTB 1090:27, FHL 0113385.
[22] J.L. Terwen, *Het Koningrijk der Nederlanden* (1858) and Dutch encyclopedia *Winkler Prins* (1975).
[23] The earliest records for the Dutch Reformed churches at Deventer are a combined *baptismal* record for the Broerenkerk and the Burgkerk, supposedly available for 1591 to 1637. The records actually begin in 1571 and run until 1579; then there is a gap to 1586, after which they run through 1637. The earliest *marriage* records available on microfilm begin in 1664.
[24] The first record of the Pier surname in the New World was 24 April 1681 at the baptism of Rachel Jans Pier's son Frans in Kingston, N.Y., where the name was recorded as Pyer. Other variations found in later records of the time were Pier, Peer, Aspeere, Spier, and Speer. The recordings Spier and Speer appear to be phonetic misrepresentations of individuals whose given names end in –s. For example, Teunis Pier, when spoken aloud, can sound like either Teunis Pier or Teunis Spier, and thus the error is obvious.
[25] Deventer Kerkelijke Registers, 1571-1637, unpaginated, FHL 0116517.

Henderick, bap. 13 Apr. 1606, sp. Hendrick van Merkelen, Henderick Geresen, fenne[26] Sijnchen; d.y.

Goert, bap. 28 March 1608, sp. Claes Ernsten, Harmen Guerts.

Margrieta, bap. 15 Apr. 1610, sp. Henderick van Haeckenbarge, Anna Van Essen, Gerreijtijen Retstap.

Hinge,[27] bap. 3 May 1612, sp. Hans Ijndenvos, Henderick Schrijner, Reijntijen Geerlichs.

Abraham, bap. 29 May 1614, sp. Hans Morre, Lijsbet Wolters.

Anneken, bap. 28 Jan. 1616, sp. Ijan Meijs Spiesemaker en frouw Bocks en De Frouwe Ijnden Vos.

Henderick, bap. 23 Mar. 1617. *De getuijgen quade.*[28]

It is possible that the Willem van Essen who sponsored the baptism of Toeniss Jansz in 1603 was the maternal grandfather, the father of Aeltijen Willems van Essen, but a search of the Deventer records available to us did not provide us with any further van Essen information.

The frequency with which the Ijnden Vos family is used as baptismal sponsors may indicate a familial relationship but we found no other mention of this name in the available Deventer records. There was no mention of Jan Pijr in the *Poerterboeken*,[29] and no other children were found for him and his wife Aeltijen.

Pier in New Netherland: Jan Theunissen. The name of Jan Theunissen's wife Maritje/Maria/Marie Jans has only been known from records in New Netherland. On 5 March 1664 Jan and Maria had a son, Theunis, baptized in the Reformed Dutch Church of New Amsterdam.[30]

The record of Jan's arrival on the *St. Jan Baptiste* on 6 August 1661 lists his wife and two children, ages 1¼ and 4 years.[31] Researchers have only been able to name one of those children — Rachel, who married Arie Fransen de Lange and Hendrick Ploeg in Kingston, New York. Rachel's patronymic of Jans and her surname Pier were known from the baptism of several of her children. The first time her full name is used is at her son Frans Ariesen de Lange's baptism 24 April 1681 in Kingston.[32] Rachel's placement as Jan and Maria's daughter is based on several supporting facts,[33] but until now, no baptismal record had been located for her.

---

26 Fenne is a Frisian name; see note following.

27 The use of the Frisian name Hinge (Hinke) may provide us with a clue to the origin of Jan Pijr.

28 A dictionary of 17th century Dutch defines *quade* as angry, evil, bad, *quadie* as rascal, criminal, villain, wrongdoer. Its meaning in connection with *de getuijgen* (the witnesses/sponsors) is not known.

29 Deventer Poerterboeken, 1595-1702, FHL 0116533.

30 *Baptisms from 1639 to 1730 in the Reformed Dutch Church, New York*, Collections of The New York Genealogical and Biographical Society, vol. 2 (1901) [hereafter *Baptisms 1639-1730*], p. 72 (Parents: Jan Teuniszen, Marrie Jans. Child: Theunis. Sponsors: Jan Spiegelsaen, Gerrit Lambertze).

31 West India Company Account Book, see note 3 above.

32 Roswell Randall Hoes, *Baptismal and Marriage Register of the Old Dutch Church of Kingston, Ulster County, New York, 1660-1809* (New York, 1891, repr. Baltimore, 1980, 1997) [hereafter *Kingston Dutch Church*], p. 14, baptism #226 (Parents: Aryan Fransen, Rachel Jansen Pyer [*sic*]).

33 Under the traditional Dutch naming pattern the first two sons would be named after the grandfathers and the first two daughters after the grandmothers. Rachel Jans Pier named her second-born son Jan and her first-born daughter Maria, which supports her placement as a daughter of Jan Teunis-

Her marriage record to her second husband Albert Hendricksen Ploeg reveals her place of birth as Amsterdam, and a search of the baptismal records there was conducted in the GAA on our behalf. Knowing that Jannetie was either the 4-year old or the 1¼-year old on board the *St. Jan Baptiste* in 1661 allowed us to narrow the search to the years 1656 to 1660. Rachel is an unusual name in the Amsterdam records and there was only one child of that name baptized to parents Jan Theunissen and Maria Jans:

> Parents: Jan Tonneis, Marike Jares.[34] Child: Raeghel. Baptized: 28 January 1660. Sponsors: Hyndrick Tonneisen, Jakob Tonneisen.[35]

We concluded that this child Rachel, baptized in 1660 in the Nieuwe Kerk, was the 1¼-year old on board the *St. Jan Baptiste* with her parents and 4-year old sibling. But we still had to find Rachel's sibling.

With their earliest known child born *circa* 1657 we could narrow the search for the marriage of Jan Theunissen and Maria Jans. Considering it unlikely that Jan Theunissen married before the age of 20 in 1651, we searched the marriage intentions from 1651 to 1657. Only two entries were found for a Jan Theunissen and Maria Jans (and variations). One was for Jan Tamese and Marritje Jeurianns from Norway, dated 3 October 1654, and this couple could be immediately eliminated due to the difference in names and place of origin. The other marriage intention that we briefly considered occurred 11 October 1657 for Jan Tueniss, age 29, from Dokkum, assisted by his uncle Jan Petersen Buerringh, and Maria Jonis from Amsterdam, age 25, assisted by her mother Grietje Jans.[36] With Dokkum as the place of origin for Jan either this was the wrong entry or the recorder had switched the places of origin for bride and groom. It was tempting to consider this marriage, but Jan Theunissen Pier also would have been 26, not 29. We had to face the possibility that Jan and Maria had married outside the city of Amsterdam.

Our search for another child baptized at Amsterdam to Jan Theunissen and Maria *circa* 1657 was also without success. Only one child could be found baptized in Amsterdam at that time to a couple with similar names, an Aeltien baptized 25 August 1658 in the Westerkerk. However, one of Aeltien's baptismal sponsors was Grietien Jans, the name of the mother of Maria Jonis from Amsterdam whose marriage intention to Jan Tueniss from Dokkum was found in 1657. We considered it likely that Aeltien was a child of the latter couple and not of Jan Theunissen Pier and Maria Jans.

---

sen and Maria Jans. Her first-born son was named Frans in honor of his paternal grandfather. There were no Jan Piers in New Netherland of an age to be Rachel's father, other than Jan Teunissen Pier.

[34] According to Monique Peters, the patronymic Teunissen can be written as Tonneis, and Jares can be another form of the patronymic Jans.

[35] Amsterdam Nieuwe Kerk Baptisms. DTB 76:185, FHL 0113146. Although these sponsors could be brothers of Jan, research has not turned up any baptismal records for them.

[36] Amsterdam Marriage Intentions, 473:468, FHL 0113209.

Since we found no child baptized *circa* 1657 to Jan and Maria in Amsterdam, we had to consider the possibility that the 4-year old child on the *St. Jan Baptiste* in 1661 had been born and baptized outside Amsterdam. Without knowing where Jan and Maria married or baptized their child we could not proceed with research in the Netherlands, so our search turned back to New Netherland and its records. The Dutch placed great importance in the choice of baptismal sponsors when a child was christened, and it was likely that if the unknown older sibling to Rachel Janse Pier lived to adulthood and married, he (or she) would use Pier relatives as sponsors at his (or her) own children's baptisms.

As previously noted, Jan Theunissen and Maria Jans arrived in New Netherland 6 August 1661 with two children, one being Rachel baptized in 1660 in Amsterdam. On 5 March 1664 a son Teunis was baptized at New Amsterdam.[37] No other children have been found for this couple in the records of New Amsterdam/New York. Sometime before 19 March 1676 Jan Theunissen Pier died, and his widow Maria married Willem Janszen Romen in New York.[38] With this marriage she assumed the role of stepmother to Romen's known sons by his first wife: *Jan Willemse Romen*, born about 1658 in Werckendam, North Brabant, The Netherlands;[39] *Pieter Willemse Romen*, baptized in New Amsterdam 20 October 1660;[40] and *Jacob Willemse Romen*, baptized in New Amsterdam 1 August 1663.[41] By 26 December 1691 Maria's second husband was dead, and she married for the third time, to Hendrick Hendricksen Obee.[42] Her marriage to Obee brought Maria at least four more step-children: *Lydia Hendricks Obee*, baptized 5 June 1658;[43] *Grietie/Margriet Hendricks Obee*, baptized 17 August 1659;[44] *Claes Hendrickse Obee*, baptized 1 May 1661;[45] and *Lysbeth Hendricks Obee* (no baptism found).

In order to search for the missing child of Jan Theunissen and Maria Jans, it was essential to have the names of all children and their spouses, including any stepchildren of Maria by her other marriages. We were looking for a man or woman with the patronymic of Jans(en), having children baptized and using as baptismal sponsors Maria Jans, her Pier

[37] *Baptisms 1639-1730*, p.72 (note 30 above).

[38] *Marriages from 1639 to 1801 in the Reformed Dutch Church, New York*, Collections of The New York Genealogical and Biographical Society, vol. 9 (1940), p. 41 ("Willem Janszen Romen, Wedr. Van Jannetje Jans, en Maritje Jans, Wede. Van Jan Theuniszen, woonende op't Versche water [living at the Fresh Water]"), first banns 19 Mar., married 12 Apr. 1676. The Fresh Water pond, also known as the *Kalck* (Collect), was north of the city wall (Wall St.) near the present City Hall.

[39] Howard S.F. Randolph, "The Rommen-Romme-van Longstraat Family and the Roome Family," REC. 64:338-39.

[40] *Baptisms 1639-1730*, p. 58.

[41] Ibid., p. 70.

[42] *Marriages from 1639 to 1801*, p. 71 ("Hendrick Obee, Wedr. V. Keltie Claes, en Marritje Jans, Wede. V. Willem Janszen, beÿde wonende alhier [both living here]," first banns 26 Dec. 1691, married 13 Jan. 1692).

[43] *Baptisms 1639-1730*, p. 49.

[44] Ibid., p. 53.

[45] Ibid., p. 60.

children or her Romen or Obee stepchildren. As well, this individual had to be of an age close to that of the unknown child age 4 in August 1661. The man or woman meeting these criteria could be the missing child. Our search proved successful.

On 5 July 1676 Jannetje Jans, from Leiden, married Jan Davidszen [DuFour] in the Reformed Dutch Church of New York.[46] Although Riker and others identified Jannetje as a daughter of Jan Willemszen Van Isselsteyn,[47] our research indicates otherwise. A close look at the children baptized to Jan and Jannetje reveals a naming pattern matching the Pier family, not the Van Isselsteyn; a preponderance of sponsors from Pier and related families; and a singular lack of any Van Isselsteyn sponsors. We also note that the naming of their first daughter Jannetje was likely in honor of Jan Theunissen Pier's mother Jannetje Arents.

Jan Willemszen Van Isselsteyn was married to Willemtje Jans, yet there is no daughter named Willemtje in the six daughters of Jan DuFour and Jannetje Jans. No children of Jan Van Isselsteyn and Willemtje Jans sponsored the baptisms of any of the twelve known children of Jan DuFour and Jannetje Jans.[48]

If Jannetje were a daughter of Jan Willemszen, her marriage intention stating she was from Leiden would mean she was born before 1650, when Jan Willemszen is first found having a child baptized in New Amsterdam.[49] This would make Jannetje at least 26 years old at her marriage to Jan DuFour, and with her last child baptized in 1701, she would be 51 years old. While it is possible for a woman that age to bear children, it is not as probable as for a younger woman.

Jannetje's residence at the time of her marriage in 1676 was "de bouwerye" (Stuyvesant's Bowery, north of the city) and we know that Jan Theunissen Pier owned land there from as early as 1667 until his widow sold it in April 1680.[50]

---

[46] *Marriages from 1639 to 1801*, p. 42 ("Jan Davidszen, j.m. Uÿt Sweden, aen de Deutelbay, en Jannetje Jans, j.d. Van Leÿden, aan de bouwerÿe," first banns 18 June, married 5 July 1676; Jan's residence "Deutelbay" was Turtle Bay, Manhattan).

[47] James Riker, *Revised History of Harlem* (New York, 1904), pp. 409-10. Riker looked for a father named Jan for Jannetje and erroneously assumed one in Jan Willemsen van Isselsteyn alias Jan Van Leyden, probably making the assumption because Jan Willemsen Van Isselsteyn was the correct age and both he and Jannetje were from Leiden. Jannetje is also erroneously attributed as a daughter of Jan Willemsen Van Isselsteyn in Thomas F. De Voe, *DeVeaux Family, Introducing the Numerous Forms of Spelling the Name by Various Branches and Generations in the Past Eleven Hundred Years* (1885), p. 19.

[48] Jan Willemszen Van Isselsteyn's children baptized at New Amsterdam were Geertruyd, Machtelt, Willem, Jacomyntje, Maria, and Cornelis (*Baptisms 1639-1730*, pp. 27, 39, 48, 63, 75, 95). Willemtje Jans or Willemtje Willems is listed as the mother in all but the first baptism, where no mother is named.

[49] *Baptisms 1639-1730*, p. 27 (Geertruyd of Jan Willemszen Yselsteÿn, 22 May 1650).

[50] "Whereas Anthony Anthony, of the Bowery aforesaid . . . stood poss'st of a certaine parcell of land . . . and the said Anthony Anthony having since sold all his right and interest to the land afore specifyed and premises unto John Theunis, deceased, the which is since devolved upon Maritie Jans, his widow, and William Jansen Roman, her present husband" (William Jansen Roman and Maritie Jans, of this city, heretofore widow of John Thuenis, of the Bowery, to the Deacons of the Reformed Church of this City, deed dated 20 Apr. 1680, N.Y. Secretary of State Deeds 6:183, cited in I.N. Phelps Stokes, *Iconography of Manhattan Island 1498-1909*, 6 vols. [1915-28], 6:150, courtesy of Howard Swain).

be from this marriage. A notation in the marriage intention indicated that Geesje had satisfied the Weeskamer on 14 October 1660, suggesting that she had children by her prior marriage to Pieter Carstense.

Record of Pieter Carstense's death and children by Geesje has now been found in the Weeskamer *Calisregister* of 14 October 1660:[59]

> *Pieter Carstens overleden in Oost Indien heeft gelaten twe kinderen doch geen middelen soo als Geesie Jans de weduwe verklaarde sulcx deselve niets voor vaders erf en kan beijsen ende welke jannetie Arens de moer*[60] *getuijgde waerachtich te zijn, P(rese)n(ti)b(us) allen de heren dempto Schellingen den 14 october 1660*

> Pieter Carstens died in the East Indies leaving behind two children with no money or possessions. Geesje Jans his widow can provide nothing to the children for their father's inheritance. Jannetie Arents, aunt [to the children], declares this to be the truth . . . 14 October 1660.

Pieter Carstens's death in the East Indies (present day Indonesia) probably means that he had gone there in the service of the East India Company.

Mr. Brooks discussed his finding of the burial of Pieter "Karstensen" in Amsterdam on 21 September 1659, but that burial record does not mention his widow by name, although it states that he left two children;[61] if Pieter Carstens[en] died in the East Indies, however, he was not buried in Amsterdam. The 14 October 1660 record is clearly that of Pieter Carstensen and his widow Geesje Jans, who married Arent Theunissen Pier that same month. While the names of the two children of Geesje Jans and Pieter Carstensen were not given in the *Calisregister*, we have their names from their baptismal records in 1654 and 1657.

The *Calisregister* record supports the previously-published evidence that the children who sailed with Geesje Jans and Arent Theunissen Pier on the *St. Jan Baptiste* in 1661 were Tryntie Pieters and Pieter Pietersen (Ostrander).

Jannetie Arents. This *Calisregister* record showed an unexpected link with the mention of Jannetie Arents as an *aunt* to the two children born to Pieter Carstensen and Geesje Jans.

This was surprising. When a widowed spouse contemplated remarriage, he or she had to ensure the rights of any children from the previous marriage. Under Dutch law, *a relative of the deceased person* had to be present to guarantee that the children's rights were protected. This means that Jannetie Arents, who would become Geesje Jans' mother-in-law when Geesje married Jannetie's son Arent Theunissen, was also related to Pieter

[59] Amsterdam Weeskamer, Calisregister, no. 108, p. 138, GAA. The Calisregister is the Weeskamer's register of individuals who died outside of Amsterdam leaving underage children in the city.
[60] According to Pim Nieuwenhuis, "moer" is a 17th century Dutch word for "aunt."
[61] "Pietersen Parentage," p. 171. In his discussion of this burial record, Mr. Brooks stated that *3 baar van 14 raef* was a reference to the grave location, but at our request this record was studied again by Monique Peters. Her interpretation, based on films in the GAA, was *1 baar van 14 (en) roef*, meaning that 14 nickels were paid for the bier (on which the coffin was carried) and an ornamental part of the lid.

certain and some only probable, because the mother's name is not given in these baptisms):

- i. *Stitgen*, (bap.) 19 Aug. 1625, sp. Folckert Pieters, Kuytgen [?Grietjen] Gerrits, Styntgen Pieters[94] [the sponsor Styntgen Pieters later married Tryntje Thyssen's brother Laurens]; d.y.
- ii. *Stitgen*, 26 July 1626, sp. Arent Jans [Kock?], Annetjen Hendricks.[95] She is named in the Weeskamer record of Pieter Carstens in 1653. She m. in Amsterdam 27 Sept. 1644 Pieter Reijnders[96] and had several children baptized in Amsterdam.
- iii. *Foltgen*, 10 Oct. 1628, sp. Lourens Teijssen [brother of Tryntje Thyssen], Anneke Cornelis, Aeltgen Lourents;[97] d.y.
- iv. *Johannes*, 8 Sept. 1630, sp. Andries Lourens, Heyndrick Stoffels, Lijntien Harmense.[98]
- v. *Marytjen*, 28 Sept. 1632, sp. Jan van der Hese, Annetje Boudewins, Selitgen Carstens.[99]
- vi. *Annetie*, 27 May 1635, sp. Cornelis Tyssen, Styntje Pieters[100] [brother and sister-in-law to Tryntje Thyssen].
- vii. *Cornelis*, 30 Aug. 1637, sp. Roelof Pietersen, Tryntjen Pieters[101] [Tryntjen possibly the same person who gave Volckgen Pieters her maternal inheritance in 1662].
- viii. *Mateus*, 20 Mar. 1640, sp. Tade Jans, [   ] Mans, Styntje Pieters [wife of Laurens Thyssen].[102]
- ix. *Vooltjen*, 16 Jan. 1643/44, sp. Tadde Jansz, Stijnte Pieters, Aeltje Willems[103] [Stijnte Pieters was the wife of Laurens Thyssen and Aeltje Willems was married to Cornelis Thyssen]. Vooltjen m. in Amsterdam (int.) 14 Oct. 1670 Dirck Hillebrantse.[104]
- x. *Volckert*, 19 Mar. 1646/47, sp. Pieter Jansz, Annitjen Jansz.[105]

The baptismal sponsors for Stitgen (1625), Foltgen (1628), Annetie (1635), Cornelis (1637), Mateus (1640) and Vooltjen (1644) allow us to place them definitely as children of Pieter Carstensen and Trijntje Thyssen, and Stitgen (1626) and Vooltjen are further confirmed by the 1654 Weeskamer record previously mentioned.

94 Amsterdam Oude Evangelisch Lutherse Kerk, Baptisms, DTB 139:137, FHL 0113415.
95 Ibid., 139:178, FHL 0113415.
96 Amsterdam Oude Evangelisch Lutherse Kerk, Marriages, FHL 0114984.
97 Amsterdam Oude Evangelisch Lutherse Kerk, Baptisms, DTB 139:247, FHL 0113415.
98 Ibid., DTB 139:365, FHL 0113415.
99 Ibid., DTB 140:34, FHL 0113415.
100 Ibid., DTB 140:158, FHL 0113415.
101 Ibid., DTB 140:242, FHL 0113416.
102 Ibid., DTB 140:38, FHL 0113416.
103 Ibid., DTB 141:166, FHL 0113416.
104 Amsterdam Marriage Intentions, 688:144, FHL 0113220 (*Dirc Hillebrantse van Amsterdam, vlotschuytvoerder, 21 jaar oud, woont op de Braak en Volckie Pieters van Amsterdam oud 21 jaar, ouders dood, geassisteerd met haar nicht Annetie Laurens, woont als boven. Beiden kunnen niet schrijven.* Translation: Dirc Hillebrantse from Amsterdam, bargeman, 21 years old, lives on the Braak, and Volckie Pieters from Amsterdam, 21 [sic] years old, her parents are dead, assisted by her cousin Annetie Laurens, [Volckie] lives at the same place [the Braak]. Both cannot write.).
105 Amsterdam Oude Evangelisch Lutherse Kerk, Baptisms, 141:426, FHL 0113416.

iii. Laurens Thyssen, b. about 1608 in Husum, m. 1632 Stijntie Pieters, widow of Jochem Hooftman.[92]

Mr. Brooks' article also detailed two probable children for Tryntje Thyssen and Pieter Carstensen — *Sytgen* baptized 1625, and *Foltgen* baptized 1628. However, further research has provided us with more children, and confirmed the identity of the two children previously found.

At Pieter's marriage to Geesje Jans in 1654, mention was made of the Weeskamer, which was responsible for ensuring the inheritance rights of underage children of a deceased person whose spouse was about to remarry. This record had not been found at the time of publication of Mr. Brooks' article, but further research conducted at the Amsterdam archives has resulted in its finding:[93]

Den 10 julu 1654 heeft Pieter Carstensz, herbergier, bewesen syn onmondige dochter Volckge out 11 jaer, daer moeder of was trijntge thijs voor haer moeders erf een somme van vijftich gld. ende sal etc. onder verband eetc dese sal jij etc ende het behaeche sytge pieters de dochter ende Styntge Pieters de moeye: presentibus de heer Johan van der Poll, etc.

Op 8 maart 1662 heeft Trijntie Pieters in voldoeninghe vant nevenstaande boven [?] deze [?] opgebracht vijftich gulden die terstont werden [?] zijn behandigd aan de voorschreven Volckgen Pieters om haar de nodighe kleederen te verschaffen.

10 July 1654 Pieter Carstensz, innkeeper, has proved that his underage daughter Volckge, 11 years old, whose mother was Trijntge Thijs, has for her maternal inheritance 50 guilders . . . [witnesses] Sytge Pieters the daughter and Styntge Pieters the aunt: presented before de Heer Johan Van der Poll, etc.

On 8 March 1662 Trijntie Pieters in satisfaction of the above has brought 50 guilders and given it directly to Volckgen Pieters to buy needed clothing.

Here we see Pieter Carstensen's child Vooltjen/Volckge baptized in 1644 (see below), although her age should be 10, not 11. Her older sister Sytge is with her but because she is not underage she does not have to have her rights ensured. This record does not preclude the possibility that more than two of the children of Pieter Carstensen and Tryntje Thyssen survived to adulthood, but further research would be required to find them. A listing of children of Pieter Carstensen and Tryntje Thyssen was compiled from baptisms in the Oude Evangelische Lutherse Kerk Amsterdam (some are

---

[92] For the marriage of Laurens Thyssen and Stijntie Pieters see "Pietersen Parentage," p. 170 note 30. They had three children baptized in the Oude Evangelische Lutherse Kerk (DTB as cited below, FHL 0113415):
   i. Vroutien, bap. 7 Aug. 1633, sp. Cornelis Tijssen [brother of Laurens], Vroutje Pieters [wife of Cornelis Tijssen] (140:70).
   ii. Annitie, bap. 13 Dec. 1636, sp. Pieter Carstens [husband of Tryntie Thyssen], Annitje Jans, Annitje Jacobs (140:208). This child Annitie is probably the Anneke Laurens named as cousin to Volckie Pieters (daughter of Pieter Carstensen and Tryntje) at her marriage to Dirc Hillebrantse in 1670.
   iii. Vooletien, bap. 2 Nov. 1638, sp. Trijntje Tijsz [sister of Laurens] (140:312).
[93] Amsterdam Weeskamer, Inbrengregisters, nr. 29, p. 165, GAA.

sponsors of Pieter and Trijntje's children at Kingston showed an unusually strong tie to the Arent Theunissen Pier family. Arent had emigrated to New Netherland in 1661 on the *St. Jan Baptiste* with a wife and two children. A check of the DTB records in Amsterdam showed that Arent Theunissen married in 1660 Geesje Jans, the widow of Pieter Carstensen. Additional research uncovered Geesje's marriage to Pieter Carstensen "van Noorstrand" in 1654 along with the births of two children: Tryntje and Pieter. It was determined that the two children on the *St. Jan Baptiste* with Arent Theunissen Pier and his wife Geesje Jans were Geesje's children from her first marriage to Pieter Carstensen, namely Tryntje Pieters and Pieter Pietersen [Ostrander].

"Pietersen Parentage" also determined that Pieter Carstensen was previously married to Tryntje Thyssen, daughter of Thys Cornelisz and Volcken Laurens, and speculated that Laurens Thyssen was a probable brother to Tryntje. Further research by the authors has uncovered another brother, Cornelis Thyssen.

The known children of Thys Cornelisz and Volcken Laurens were:

    i. Tryntje Thyssen,[88] b. about 1605 in Husum,[89] m. Pieter Carstensen.[90]

    ii. Cornelis Thyssen, b. about 1604 in Husum, m. three times in Amsterdam: (1) 1639 to Vroutje Pieters, sister of Stijntie Pieters (wife of Cornelis' brother Laurens Thyssen), (2) 1643 to Aaltje Willems, (3) 1662 to Giertje Egberts.[91]

---

88 "Pietersen Parentage" noted two death records for a Tryntje Thyssen, in 1635 and 1636. With the finding that she had more children baptized as late as 1646/47, and her husband's remarriage in 1654, we can narrow her date of death to between March 1646/47 and July 1654.

89 Although her marriage intention of 18 Feb. 1623 as found in Amsterdam DTB 427:423 gives her place of origin as Noorstrand and her bridegroom Pieter Carstens' as Husum, it is most probable that an error was made by the recording clerk and the origins reversed. Tryntje's brothers were from Husum and it is probable that she was as well.

90 "Pietersen Parentage" gave the 18 Feb. 1623 marriage intention in full but omitted the notation *4 ans* [4 years] after "met Mathijs Michels sijn bekender" and also after "tryn thijsen van Noorstrand out 18 jaeren." Thus the document reveals that both Pieter Carstensz and Tryntje Thijsen had been in Amsterdam for four years; given their ages, they both most likely arrived with parents or older siblings.

91 Cornelis' first (1639) marriage intention reads: Cornelis Tijssen from Housum, sailor, residing in the Goudsbloemstraat, having no parents, and Vroutje Pieters from Amsterdam, 23 years of age, residing as before [also in the Goudsbloemstraat], having no parents, assisted by Stijntie Pieters her sister. Cornelis' second marriage intention dated 25 July 1643 reads: Cornelis Thijssen from Amsterdam, sailor, widower of Vroutje Pieters, and Aaltje Willems, from Amsterdam, 22 years of age, assisted by Susanna Jans her mother. The third marriage intention of Cornelis was dated 2 April 1662 and reads: Cornelis Thyssen from Hoesum, schuisdeoris? [occupation], widower of Aeltje Willems, [living] by the Zuterdeeghtbrug, and Grietie Egberts van Koor, widow of Jacob Harmens, [living] by the Koornsluis (Amsterdam Marriage Intentions, 451:83 [church]; 459:328 [church] also 677:134 [Pui], 685:138 [Pui].).

Children of Cornelis Thyssen and Aaltje Willems baptized in the Oude Evangelische Lutherse Kerk, Amsterdam (DTB as cited below, FHL 0113416):

i. Vooletjen, bap. 5 Dec. 1645, sp. Hendrick Jansen, Trijntjen Tijssen [sister of Cornelis], Greit Jans (141:313).

ii. Hendricus, bap. 2 Mar. 1649, sp. Pieter Carstensen [husband of Tryntje Thyssen], Pieter Jans, Marten Michielsen (142:114).

iii. Willem, bap. 21 Mar. 1649, listed three lines below Hendricus, above, with no indication the boys were twins, sp. Pieter Carstensen [see above], Pieter Jans, Maritie Michielsen (142:114).

iv. Matijs, bap. 8 Dec. 1650, sp. Matijs Michiels, Man--enes Willems, Tryntie Tijssen [sister of Cornelis] (142:242).

iv. Teunis Arentsen Pier, bap. between 21 May and 21 Aug. 1670 in Hurley, Ulster Co., N.Y.,[81] m. 5 July 1702 in Kingston Margaret/Grietje Du Foe/Dufour,[82] bap. 5 Nov. 1681 in New York City.[83] She was the daughter of Jannetje Jans Pier and Jan Dufour and thus Teunis' first cousin once removed.

Children of Pieter Carstensen and Geesje Jans:[84]

i. Tryntje Pieters, prob. bap. 15 Dec. 1654 in the Amsterdam Lutheran Church, m. Hendrick Albertsen Ploegh and resided at Kingston.[85]
ii. Pieter Pietersen (Ostrander), bap. 3 July 1657 in the Amsterdam Lutheran Church, m. Rebecca Traphagen 19 Jan. 1679 at Kingston.[86]

OSTRANDER UPDATE

"Pietersen Parentage" published in 1999[87] dispelled the myth that Pieter Pietersen, an adelborst (cadet) from Amsterdam, was the ancestor of the Ostrander family. Interested readers will find a complete and fully documented account of the corrected Ostrander family lineage in "Pietersen Parentage," but a brief explanation is in order. The lineage that was formerly claimed started with Pieter Pietersen the adelborst, who arrived in New Netherland in 1660 as part of a group of soldiers on the *Bonte Koe* with a wife and three children ages 8, 4 and 2. This unsubstantiated lineage identified the three children as Peter (whose descendants used the surname Ostrander), Tryntje (who married Hendrick Albertsen Ploeg) and Geesje (who married a Jan Pier). A Tryntje van de Lande had also been accepted in previously published genealogies as the mother of these three children, and wife to Pieter Pietersen, adelborst.

Unfortunately the previously claimed lineage of the Ostrander family could not be proven. An attempt made to verify the story through research in the Amsterdam DTB records proved unsuccessful, but a study of the

---

78 *Kingston Dutch Church*, p. 6, baptism #91 (Parents: Arent Tuenesse, Geesjen Jans. Child: Gepje. Sponsors: Hendrick Jochemsen and his wife).

79 *Kingston Dutch Church*, p. 508 marriage #73 (Hendrick Adriaanz, j.m. of Gelderland residing in Kingston, and Gepie Arentz Pier, j.d. born in Kingston and residing there; first banns 3 Jan. 1684/5).

80 *Kingston Dutch Church*, p. 514, marriage #145 (Willem Trephagen, widower of Tryntje Peele, and Gepje Pier, widow of Hendrick Ariaanse, both residing in Kingston; married before Jan Tysse).

81 *New York Historical Manuscripts: Dutch, Kingston Papers*, 2 vols., transl. Dingman Veersteeg (Baltimore: Genealogical Publishing Co., 1976), 2:739. His baptism is recorded in the official papers of the Kingston Secretary between the 21 May and 21 August entries.

82 *Kingston Dutch Church*, p. 519, marriage #194 (Teunis Pier, j.m. born in Horle [Hurley] and residing in Kingstouwn [Kingston], and Margriet du Foer, j.d. born and residing in N. Jorck [New York]; banns published but dates not given).

83 *Baptisms 1639-1730*, p. 149.

84 For more information see "Pietersen Parentage," pp. 163-73.

85 No marriage record has been found but baptisms of this couple's children occur in the Kingston Dutch Church.

86 *Kingston Dutch Church*, p. 504, marriage #36 (Pieter Pietersse, y.m. of Amsterdam, and Rebecca Traphaghe, y.d. of Boswyck [Bushwick, L.I.], both residing in Westquansengh; banns published three times but dates not given).

87 See note 1, above.

Children of Jan Theunisz Pier and Maritje/Maria Jans:

    i.   Jannetje[2] Jans Pier, bap. 12 Aug. 1657 in the Marekerk, Leiden, Neth., m. Jan Davidsen DuFour 5 July 1676 in New York City.

    ii.   Rachel Jans Pier, bap. 28 Jan. 1660 in Amsterdam, d. abt. 1723 in N.Y. She m. (1) Arie Franssen De Lange abt. 1677 in Ulster Co., N.Y.,[67] he d. bef. 1699 in Kingston, Ulster Co. She m. (2) Albert Hendrickszen Ploeg 17 Apr. 1699 in Kingston, he was b. Kingston.[68]

    iii. Teunis Jansen Pier, bap. 5 Mar. 1664 in New Amsterdam,[69] d. bef. 9 Apr. 1729 in Newark, Essex Co., N.J.[70] He m. Catrina Tomasse [probably Cadmus] 6 Oct. 1684 in Bergen, N.J.,[71] bap. 2 Sept. 1662 in New Amsterdam,[72] d. 27 Apr. 1748 in Bergen.[73].

4. ARENT[1] THEUNISZ PIER (Theunis[A] Jansz, Jan[B]) was baptized 27 December 1637 in Amsterdam, and died after 1703 in Kingston, Ulster County, New York. He married, 31 October 1660 in Amsterdam, GEESJE JANS, daughter of Jan Doets and widow of Pieter Carstensen. She was born about 1630 in Norden, Ostfriesland, Germany, and died after 1703 in Kingston.

Children of Arent Theunisz Pier and Geesje Jans:

    i.   Harmen[2] Arentsen Pier, bap. 10 Aug. 1661 in New Amsterdam,[74] no marriage known.

    ii.   Jannetie Arents Pier, bap. 12 July 1664 in Kingston,[75] m. Jan. 1681/82 in Kingston. Pieter Pieterse Winne,[76] bap. 20 Nov. 1661 Kingston.[77]

    iii. Gepie Arents Pier, bap. 25 Mar. 1668 Kingston,[78] m. (1) 19 Jan. 1684/85 in Kingston, Hendrick Adriaanz, b. Gelderland, Neth.,[79] d. bef. 1699 in Kingston. She m. (2) Willem Traphagen 30 Apr. 1699 in Kingston.[80]

---

[67] While no marriage record has been found, children of this couple were baptized in the Kingston Dutch Church, and Rachel's marriage to her second husband names her as the widow of Arie Franssen.

[68] *Kingston Dutch Church*, p. 514, marriage #143 (Allert Hendricksen Ploeg, j.m. born and residing in Kingstouwn, and Rachel Pier, widow of Arie Franssen, born in Amsterdam and residing here in Kingstouwn). Allert [Albert] was the son of Hendrick Ploeg and Tryntje Pieters [Ostrander].

[69] *Baptisms 1639-1730*, p. 72.

[70] Will of Tunis Pier dated 1 Oct. 1727 proved 9 Apr. 1729 (*Calendar of New Jersey Wills*, vol. 1, New Jersey Archives, First Series, vol. 23 [1901], pp. 364-65, abstracting N.J. Wills B:119).

[71] Teunis Jansen Spier [*sic*], y.m. from New York, and Catharyna Thomasse, y.d. from Bergen, first banns 14 Sept., m. 6 Oct. by the minister at Bergen (Dingman Versteeg and Thomas E. Vermilye Jr., *Bergen Records, Records of the Reformed Protestant Dutch Church of Bergen in New Jersey 1666 to 1788* [reprinted Baltimore: Genealogical Publishing Co., 1976, from *Year Book of the Holland Society of New York* 1913-1915], 3 vols. in 1, 2:63, #65).

[72] *Baptisms 1639-1730*, p. 66, baptized as Tryntje.

[73] Versteeg and Vermilye, *Bergen Records*, 3:44, #391.

[74] *Baptisms 1639-1730*, p. 61 (Parents: Arent Theuniszen, Geesje Jans. Child: Harmen. Sponsor: Mr. Evert Pieterszen [Keteltas]). Although Harmen was baptized in New Netherland, it is most likely that he was born on board the *St. Jan Baptiste*. The ship left the Netherlands 9 May 1661, arriving in New Amsterdam on 6 August, only four days before Harmen's baptism.

[75] *Kingston Dutch Church*, p. 3, baptism #39 (Parents: Arent Tuenesse, Giesjen Jans. Child: Jannetjen. Sponsors: Jan Willemsen Hoochteylingh, Barber Jans, Lowies Duboey).

[76] *Kingston Dutch Church*, p. 506, marriage #51 (Pieter Winnen, junior, j.m. born in W. Indien [West Indies] in Curassauw [Curaçao] and residing under the jurisdiction of Kingston, and Jannetie Arentsdr. Pier, j.d. born in the Esopus under the jurisdiction of Kingston and residing there. First banns 5 Jan. 1681/2, marriage date not given).

[77] *Kingston Dutch Church*, p. 2, baptism # 11.

GENEALOGICAL SUMMARY
(except as indicated, sources are cited above)

1. JAN[B] PIJR [Pier/Pijer/Peer] was possibly of Frisian origin but was located at Deventer, Overijssel. He is not found in the *Poerterboeken* of Deventer which begin in 1595. He married before 1603 AELTIJEN WILLEMS VAN ESSEN, the daughter of Willem van Essen and _____.

Children of Jan Pijr and Aeltijen Willems van Essen, all baptized at Deventer, Overijssel:[64]

2   i.   Toeniss, bap. 1 May 1603.
     ii.   Jan, bap. 23 Sept. 1604.
     iii. Henderick, bap. 13 Apr. 1606.
     iv.   Goert, bap. 28 Mar. 1608.
     v.   Margrieta, bap.15 Apr. 1610.
     vi.   Hinge, bap. 3 May 1612.
     vii. Abraham, bap. 29 May 1614.
     viii. Anneken, bap. 28 Jan. 1616.
     ix.   Henderick, bap. 23 Mar. 1617.

2. TOENISS/THEUNIS[A] JANSZ [PIJR/PIER] (Jan[B]) was baptized 1 May 1603 in Deventer, Overijssel. He married on 6 October 1624 in Amsterdam JANNETIE ARENTS, born about 1602 possibly in Tonning, Schleswig-Holstein, daughter of Arent Joosten and (probably) Marrij Willems.[65]

Children of Theunis Jansz [Pier] and Jannetie Arents, all baptized in Amsterdam:[66]

     i.   Maerijtjen Theunis, bap. 7 Sept. 1625, probably d. young.
     ii.   Willem Theunisz, bap. 4 July 1627, no further record.
     iii. Jan Theunisz, bap. 13 Nov. 1629, probably d. young.
3   iv.   Jan[1] Theunisz Pier, bap. 19 Oct. 1631, d. before Apr. 1676 in New York.
     v.   Maritje Theunis, bap. 26 Feb. 1634, no further record.
4   vi.   Arent[1] Theunisz Pier, bap. 27 Dec. 1637, d. after 1703 in Kingston, Ulster Co., N.Y.

3. JAN[1] THEUNISZ PIER (Theunis[A] Jansz, Jan[B]) was baptized 19 October 1631 in Amsterdam, and died before April 1676 in New York. He married MARITJE/MARIA JANS before 1657 in the Netherlands. She was born about 1632 and died after 1686 in New York, having twice remarried.

---

64 Deventer Kerkelijke Registers, 1571-1637, unpaged, FHL 0116517; see above, pp. 167-68, for the sponsors to these baptisms.

65 Arent Joosten was born ca.1575 at Nieuwveen, and ca.1602 lived at Teunen, possibly present-day Tonning in Schleswig-Holstein. He married (1) Marrij Willems, who died before 1624. He married (2) by Amsterdam marriage intention dated 11 May 1624 Baertje Claes, widow of Dirck Hendricksen. Arent was dead prior to 20 Apr. 1641 when Baertje, as his widow, recorded her intention to marry Jan Volckertss.

66 For sources and sponsors see above, p. 165.

Carstensen. Her relationship to Pieter was such that she was called "aunt" to his children by Geesje. The fact that Jannetie may have been from Tonning, which is only about 25 miles from Pieter's homeplace of Nordstrand,[62] adds to the possibility of a familial relationship.

But how was Jannetie Arents an aunt to the children of Pieter Carstensen and Geesje Jans? She was born about 1602 and Pieter about 1605, according to their respective marriage intentions. Jannetie could not be a half-sister to Pieter because her father, Arent Joostens, was still alive at her marriage to Theunis Jansz in 1624, and his wife Marrij Willems, who almost certainly was Jannetie's mother, was probably alive until about 1623, as Arent remarried the following year.

We considered the possibility that Jannetie's husband Theunis Jansz died and she married a brother of Pieter Carstensen, and could thus be called aunt to Pieter's children. With this in mind, a search was made of the Amsterdam records for a possible second marriage of Jannetie. While we did find one record of a Jannetie Arents marrying a man with the patronymic of Carstense, it was rejected because the Jannetie in the marriage dated 1656 was 21 years old and thus much too young to be the same woman married to Theunis Jansz in 1624. The man in this record likewise was found not to be a brother of Pieter Carstensen.[63]

While some might argue that another Jannetie Arents was the aunt named in the Weeskamer record, we found no other Jannetie Arents of an age to be this person, except Jannetie Arents wife of Theunis Jansz.

This record wherein Jannetie Arents is named as aunt to Tryntie and Pieter Pietersen (the children of Pieter Carstensen and Geesje Jans) cannot be dismissed. Although our research did not reveal the exact nature of the relationship, that she was related to Pieter Carstensen seems clear.

Summary. Our research indicates that the two children who sailed with Jan Theunissen Pier and wife Maritie Jans on the *St. Jan Baptiste* were almost certainly Jannetje (age 4) who married Jan DuFour and Rachel baptized 1660 (age 1¼). Our research supports the previous conclusion that the two children sailing on this same ship with Arent Theunissen Pier and wife Geesje Jans were Geesje's children by her previous marriage to Pieter Carstensen, namely Tryntje probably baptized 1654 (7 years old) and Pieter baptized 1657 (4 years old).

Our research confirmed that the parents of Jan Theunissen Pier and his brother Arent Theunissen Pier were Theunis Jansz and Jannetie Arents. Jannetie's parents were Arent Joosten and probably Marrij Willems, and Theunis Jansz's parents were Jan Pijr and Aeltijen Willems van Essen.

---

62 "Pietersen Parentage," p. 169.

63 Jochem Carstense Houtman from Amsterdam, house-carpenter, 26 years old, parents dead, assisted by Waligh Hendriks, and Jannetie Arents from Amsterdam, 21 years old, assisted by ---au Lantjes [?] her mother (Amsterdam Marriage Intentions, 476:256, dated 24 Aug. 1656).

Research was undertaken in the baptismal records of the three Dutch Reformed Churches in Leiden between 1655 and 1600, looking for a Jannetje, daughter of a Jan Theunissen and Marritje Jans.[55] One baptism was located in the Marekerk for such a child:[56]

Den xij Augustus 1657

| Janneken | Jan Teunissen | Abram Abramse, Tomas Jorise |
| | Marriken Jans | Anneken Jans, Cathalyntje Lucasdr |

This child would have been almost four on 6 August 1661 when Jan Theunissen arrived on the *St Jan Baptiste*, and almost 19 in July 1676 when Jannetje Jans from Leiden married Jan Davidszen in New York. Coupled with the naming pattern used and the large number of Pier family baptismal sponsors for her children, there seems little doubt that this Jannetje Jans is indeed the daughter of Jan Theunissen Pier.

Pier in New Netherland: Arent Theunissen. On 28 April 1661 Arent Theunissen visited Notary H. Schaef in Amsterdam and signed a contract with Dirck de Wolff, broker in Amsterdam. De Wolff enlisted Arent Theunisz, blacksmith from Amsterdam, to sail with his wife to New Netherland on the ship *St. Jan (St. Jan Baptiste)*. Arent was to go to 's Gravesande [Gravesend, Long Island], to build a salt kettle, and to boil the salt day and night. Arent, his wife, and children would live rent-free and have their meals free until the end of 1662. His wages were to be 15 carolus guilders per month and if business went well he would earn 20 carolus guilders per month. Mr. Evert Pietersz. [Keteltas] would be the director and would decide if Arent was to receive a raise in pay. Evert Pietersz. was also to sell the salt in the Manhattans.[57]

The marriage intention of Arent Theunissen was previously published in Mr. Brooks' "Pietersen Parentage." Dated 2 October 1660, it stated that Arent Teunis from Amsterdam, locksmith of 21 years, assisted by his mother Jannetie Arents, intended to marry Geesje Jans from Norden, widow of Pieter Carstense.[58] Since Arent and Geesje did not marry until 1660, the two children ages 7 and 4 who sailed with them in 1661 could not

---

55 In addition, two other baptisms were located in Leiden for children of a Jan Teunissen, both in the Hooglandschekerk. One in 1654 was with a wife named Kien Claes and the second in 1658 had no wife named and was only nine months after the 1657 baptism of Janneken. Neither of these baptisms seemed credible as an additional child of Jan and Marritje.

56 Leiden, Zuid Holland, Marekerk Baptisms, unpaged, FHL 0536857?.

57 Amsterdam Notarial Archives, Inv. 1364, p. 60 (Notary H. Schaef), GAA. The inhabitants of Gravesend, mostly English, considered the land being used for the salt venture as their common meadow. The workmen of Dirck de Wolff were constantly menaced and threatened by the inhabitants, and de Wolff complained to the West India Company in Amsterdam that the English had destroyed a house and garden and pulled down fences. The salt venture ended in failure. See Drs. C.H. Jansen, "Geschiedenis van de familie de Wolff [History of the de Wolff Family]," *57th Yearbook of the Society Amstelodamum* (1964), translation courtesy of Cor Snabel. See also Jaap Jacobs, *Een zegenrijk gewest: Nieuw-Nederland in de zeventiende eeuw* (Amsterdam: Prometheus/Bert Bakker, 1999), pp. 208-09, translation courtesy of Monique Peters.

58 "Pietersen Parentage," p. 168; Amsterdam Marriage Intentions, 481:230, FHL 0113213.

The facts do not support Jannetje Jans as a daughter of Jan Willemszen Van Isselsteyn, but they do support her as a daughter of Jan Theunissen Pier. The 4-year old sailing on *St. Jan Baptiste* in 1661 would be 19 in 1676 when Jannetje Jans married, and 44 in 1701 when her last child was born.

To illustrate our belief that Jannetje Jans was the daughter of Jan Theunissen Pier and Maria Jans, the following chart shows the baptisms of her children and the relationship of baptismal sponsors to Jan and Maria. All the baptisms occurred in the New York Dutch Reformed Church[51] unless otherwise indicated. Jannetje Jans' husband Jan Davidszen was the son of David DuFour and Maria Boulyn,[52] and the traditional naming pattern is evident in the naming of the children.

Date of Baptism	Child's Name	Baptismal Sponsors
2 May 1677	Maria [mothers of Jan and Jannetje were both named Maria]	Jan Homs, *Maria Jans [widow of Jan Theunissen Pier]*
29 May 1680	Jan [named in honor of Jannetje Jans' father]	*Jan Willemszen [Romeyn] [stepson of Maria Jans]*, Appolonia Cornelis
5 Nov. 1681	Margriet	*Pieter Willemszen [Romeyn] [stepson of Maria Jans]*, Debora Jans
31 Mar. 1683	David [named in honor of Jan DuFour's father]	David Davidszen, *Rachel Jans [Pier] [daughter of Maria Jans]*
3 Feb. 1686	Pieter	*Jacob Willemszen [Romeyn] [stepson of Maria Jans]*, Magdalena Jans
23 Feb. 1687	Rachel [named in honor of Rachel Jans Pier?]	Glaude Dufourt [half-brother to Jan DuFour], Anneken Jans
21 Nov. 1688	Ariaentie	Theunis Idenszen, Anneken Claes
28 Feb. 1690	Jannetje [named in honor of Jan DuFour's stepmother or Jannetje Jans' grandmother?]	*Willem Janszen [Romeyn], Maria Jans [his wife, formerly Pier]*
6 June 1693[53]	Elizabeth	Jean Thomasen, Jeanne Janson
12 Feb. 1696	Theunis [named in honor of Jannetje Jans' brother Teunis Janse Pier or her grandfather?]	Theunis Corneliszen, *Margariet Obe [stepdaughter of Maria Jans]*
say 1698	Willem[54]	
11 May 1701	Abraham	*Theunis Janse Pier [son of Maria Jans]*, Marretje van Breme

[51] *Baptisms 1639-1730*, pp. 127, 142, 149, 158, 172, 178, 188, 196, 233, 275.

[52] The will of David DuFour and wife Jannetje Frans written 14 Sept. 1671 names their sons David, Pieter and Glaude "and a son Jan by the first wife Maria Boulyn" (Berthold Fernow, *Calendar of Wills on file and recorded in . . . Albany . . .* [1896], p. 97).

[53] Born 13 May, bap. 6 June in the French Church, N.Y.C. (*Registers of the Births, Marriages and Deaths of the "Eglise Françoise à la Nouvelle York" from 1688 to 1804*, ed. Rev. Alfred V. Wittmeyer, Colls. of the Huguenot Society of America, 1886, repr. Baltimore: Genealogical Publishing Co., 1968, pp. 28, 33).

[54] Willem's baptismal record has not been found, but he is named in the will of his father Jan DuFour (will of John DeVoer, dated 24 July 1717, proved 13 Apr. 1724; *Abstracts of Wills on File in the Surrogate's Office, City of New York*, 17 vols., Collections of The New-York Historical Society 1892-1908, 2:287-88, abstracting N.Y. Co. Wills 19B:454).

John Peer & His Wife, the Widow of Thomas Millard

JOHN PEER BORN CIRCA 1764 NEW JERSEY DIED 1808 UPPER CANADA MARRIED THE WIDOW OF THOMAS MILLARD, WHO WAS POSSIBLY SUSANNA SMOKE

John Peer, son of Jacob and Anne, is an enigma. He came to Upper Canada in 1788, married the widow of the Loyalist Thomas Millard (who may have been Susannah Smoke), lived in Ancaster, and died there unexpectedly in 1808. His children's names are unknown, although it is thought that one was Susannah Peer who married James Wedge.

It has been difficult to find details on John Peer, other than scattered and contradictory records in Ontario. His will is recorded in an index to wills for the Niagara area but it is missing from the microfilmed records. For many years I hunted for John's will, believing that if it were indexed, it had to exist somewhere. In September 2000 I filed a request to have the original will boxes at the Ontario Archives checked. Archives staff agreed that I had not simply overlooked the microfilmed will and so a search of the will boxes was conducted. A few hours later I held the will box on my lap. The original documents were there. John did not have a will but other documents had been filed in its place. These included an affidavit from Levi Peer who stated he was *"the eldest brother of John Piere"* [sic], an inventory of John's effects taken by Levi and Edward Peer and other documents concerning John's death. This very important piece of evidence provides proof of John and Levi both being sons of Jacob and further circumstantial evidence pointing to Edward being another son.

In the Miliary "C" Records there is an Abraham Peer; a David Peer; an Edward Peer and a John Peer shown as Privates in the 3 Battalion, New Jersey Volunteers. [22] A notation states that John Peer deserted 18 Feb 1788. John Peer, the son of Jacob, came to Ontario from New Jersey in 1788 and he had close ties to Edward Peer who was most probably his brother. It is possible this Private John Peer who deserted in February 1788 is our John Peer. It would explain his early arrival date of 1788, which is eight years before his father Jacob arrived.

In his Upper Canada Land Petition dated 1795 John claimed he was a minor during the American Revolution. This would put John's age at under 16 in 1773.

John further stated in his 1795 petition that his wife was the widow of Thomas Millard of Butler's Rangers. I have checked dozens of petitions without finding reference to her as other than the wife of Thomas Millard. Thomas Millard has also proven difficult to trace, and there is a further complication in names regarding Thomas Millard and a man named Thomas Miller.

In response to John's 1795 petition, the courts rejected it, and the Land Books reveal that the courts decided that John Peer's wife was not the daughter of a Loyalist as John had claimed, thus the land he wanted as a Loyalist grant to his wife, was not granted.

In 1797 John petitioned for land again, claiming he had a family and had been in *"the Province"* (Upper Canada) for nine years. This puts his year of arrival at 1788 which fits with the known facts. He was recommended for 200 acres, but he must not have taken advantage of this grant, for in December of 1798 John wrote a letter asking that Malon Bray be allowed to select his land on his behalf. He said in this letter that distance and time of year made it impossible for him to do this himself. There is no letter or follow-up on file to indicate the answer to his plea.

In 1802 John purchased 200 acres of land in Ancaster on Lot 54, Concession 2. This land was beside the land purchased by his father Jacob. By February 1808 John was dead. In the documents found in the Will Box at the Ontario Archives, there is nothing to indicate that John had a family, and Levi claims that he is the next of kin. I cannot reconcile this with the land petitions where John states he has a family unless his family has died, left him or grown up and moved away. There are no other John Peer males in the vicinity and so we cannot explain it by saying there are two different men. There seems to be only one John Peer in Upper Canada at this time.

According to researcher Valarie Albert, a John Henry Peer married Susannah Smoke and had a daughter Susan (Susannah) Peer born 4 August 1785 in Ancaster. Since our John did not arrive in Upper Canada until 1788, this may be an error in birth year. Susan (Susannah) Peer married James Wedge on 4 December 1807 in Upper Canada.

I have found no proof to definitively place any Peer individuals as his children. For now I present my research in hopes that a reader of this genealogy will have further clues or be able to place a child with John as father.

I have a theory. I suggest that Abigail Peer who married Elizabeth Marical's brother William was the daughter of Levi's brother John Peer who died in 1808 and that Levi and Elizabeth took her in after John died.

WHAT DO WE KNOW ABOUT ABIGAIL PEER?

- Abigail was born before 1800 (as per having a son in 1815) probably in Ontario.
- She married Elizabeth Marical's brother William Marical sometime before 1815.
- William and Abigail lived in Lobo, Middlesex County Ontario until her death in 1835.

- She and William had 8 children, among them a son named John and a daughter named Susannah.
- Her first born son was named Levi Peer Marical.
- Abigail died in Middlesex County Ontario in 1835.

WHAT DO WE KNOW ABOUT JOHN PEER?

- In 1795 he stated he was too young to fight in the American Revolution which began in 1775. Other facts suggest his year of birth was circa 1762 which fits with his statement that he was too young to fight in 1775.
- Levi Peer was his older brother (as per the affidavit from Levi, Stephen and Edward Peer in 1808)
- In 1795 John Peer stated he was married to the widow of a soldier named Thomas Millard or Miller who had been in Butler's Rangers. Research has not yet turned up the first name of Thomas Millard's wife. I suggest that Thomas Millard's widow was Susannah Smoke based on details from William Wedge's letter of 1890 which speaks of his great-grandparents Susannah Smoke and John Henry Peer.
- In 1797 John submitted a petition for land saying he had a wife and family.
- John died in 1808 without a will. No wife or children were named in the affidavit submitted by Levi and Edward, his brothers. It is possible that his wife was deceased.
- In 1890 William Wedge stated that his grandmother was Susan Pear [sic] the daughter of John Peer and Susannah Smoke, and that she married James Wedge. James Wedge signed Jacob Peer Sr's will as a witness.

WHAT DO WE KNOW ABOUT THOMAS MILLARD OR MILLER?

- He was dead by 1795 (Re John Peer's 1795 petition)
- He was a soldier in Butler's Rangers (Re John Peer's 1795 petition)

I have searched through land petitions and other documents for Thomas Millard or Miller and found the following:

- A Thomas Millar, farmer, petitioned in Niagara for land in 1796. He was in Kings Royal Yorkers. We can eliminate him as a candidate
- A Thomas Miller petitioned in Niagara for land in 1797. He stated his father Peter Miller was in Butler's Rangers. We can eliminate him as a candidate
- A Thomas Millard Sr. of Crowland, filed a petition 24 July 1795 and stated he arrived in "the Province" in 1777. He says he was granted 200 acres but wants 200 more acres. He was granted the extra land. He is not a candidate as the date of John Peer's petition in which he states he married the widow of Thomas Millard was 17th of July 1795
- A Thomas Millard filed a petition in 1797 in which he states he is the son of Isaiah Millard who died 5 years earlier. He signs as Thomas Millard Jr.

Usually this indicates a man's father had the same name but his father's name is clearly written as Isaiah. He is not a candidate but I am intrigued by the fact that his father died circa 1792. Could there be a mixup in first names? Or was he called Jr. to distinguish him from an uncle with the same name?

- There is a 29 year old Thomas Millard in a 1783 "census" of Niagara with his parents Thomas and Mary and siblings. He is the most likely candidate but because early Ontario records are scarce, nothing more has been found to indicate if he married. Unsourced online Family Trees state this Thomas Millard son of Thomas and Mary, died in Niagara area in 1789 which fits perfectly with his widow (if he had one) marrying John Peer.

MY THEORY

I suggest that Abigail Peer was another daughter of John Peer who died in 1808 and that this John Peer was married to Susannah Smoke. Abigail's naming of a son John and a daughter Susannah supports this theory. I believe Abigail lived with Levi and Ellizbeth after her father's death and this would account for her naming a son Levi Peer Marical.

- Abigail had to be born before 1800 but was probably born between 1795 and 1800. She would only be 8 to 13 years old in 1808 when her father died. If her mother Susanna was also deceased, she almost certainly went to live with a family member. Perhaps Levi and Elizabeth took her in to their home and that is why she is in the 1820 census and why she named her son Levi Peer Marical in honour of her uncle Levi who raised her.
- She would have easily met her future husband William Marical since he was Levi's brother-in-law and could have been a frequent visitor to the home.
- Although she was married and had 2 young children in Ontario when the 1820 census was taken in New York, Abigail may have been visiting. There are several reasons I can think of for her to make the trip -
  - perhaps someone in the family was seriously ill and Abigail made the trip to see them
  - perhaps she and her husband were having marital problems and she needed a break
  - perhaps she was missing the family she grew up with
  - perhaps she was seeking better medical treatment for her third pregnancy. Lobo, Middlesex County Ontario was just opening for settlement in 1820 and available doctors and neighbours would have been sparse. As an example, the population of the current city of London which was the largest settlement area in Middlesex County, was only 133 in 1828

SUMMARY

I stress that this is a working theory. I have not found absolute proof, but I have presented circumstantial evidence that helps support my theory. More research should be conducted to either prove or disprove that John Peer was married to Susanna Smoke and that Abigail was their daughter. Interested descendants must be cautious to not take my theory as proven fact.

TIMELINE:

1788: John Peer settled in Upper Canada (present day Ontario)

1795, 17 July: John Peer petition states he was a minor during the American Revolution but he and his family were loyal to the Crown. Nathaniel Petit vouched for the family's loyalty in an affidavit dated 16 July 1795 at Newark. Nathaniel also vouched for Jacob Peer Sr's loyalty when he applied for land.

John Peer states he is married to the widow of Thomas Millard who served in Butler's Rangers. Prays for 200 acres for himself and a further grant for his wife, and the lands of her deceased husband. Recommended for 200 acres for himself but "it does not appear that his wife has been the daughter of a UE Loyalist" Entered page 52 Land Book B [23]

Peer, John - Newark 1795 UCLP P2/46 Vol 400 C-2489 In his petition John Peer states that he was a minor at the time of warfare between America and Great Britian but loyal to His Majesty. Nathl Pett..y [Pettit] vouches for family loyalty. John Peer married the widow of Thomas Millare [sic] of C. Butler's Rangers (also, daughter of UE?) Wants land for himself and for her. Newark 1795.

1797, 13 July: John Peer of Ancaster petitioned for 200 acres of land stating he had been nine years in the Province and had a family, and had never received any certificate or order of Council for land. [24]

1797: Land Book "B" 1794-1797 p. 46 #62 states that John Peer was *"recommended for 200 acres for himself but it does not appear that his wife has been the daughter of a UE Loyalist"*

Upper Canada Land Book C 1st July, 1797 - 31st July, 1797
p. 81 Peer, John - Praying for lands as a settler. Recommended for 200 acres. [25]

1798 December 8: John Peer of Ancaster wrote a letter to William Smith asking that Malon Bray be allowed to locate 200 acres of land for him. He states there is a warrant for the land which Mr. Dixon left at his office - further stating that the distance and time of year make it difficult for him to come in person.

1800: John Peer's name is found in the Rousseau Store Ledger in Ancaster Tp.

1802: John Peer bought a 200 acre parcel from Henry Young of Concession 2 Lot 54 Ancaster Township John sold this land to Levi Peer sometime after 1802

9 February 1808: Petition of Livi Pierre [sic] *"..that John Pierre, your Petitioner's brother, died as your petitioner believes, without a last will and testament, your* *petitioner being the older brother and next of kin to the deceased..."* Signed Levi Peer, Niagara. Richard Hatt and Levi Peer swear to administer the estate.

9 February 1808: Levi Peer, Richard Hatt, Edward Peer and Stephen Peer *"all of the County of Lincoln"* paid 1000 £ to bind themselves to make a true inventory of the estate of John Peer. Signatures included. Inventory included

THE SMUCK FAMILY

Jacob and **Mary Smuck** came to Canada from the United States in about 1795. They took an oath of allegiance and settlement on 25 June, 1797. They farmed in Glandford Township, Wentworth County, Ontario, from 1796 and obtained the land as an Upper Canada land patent in 1811.

Various references record the family name as **Smuck**, **Schmuck**, **Smock**, **Smooke**, **Smoke** and **Smoak**. It appears that most of the later descendants use the name **Smuck**. The Upper Canada Land Petition records Jacob's request for Concession 4, Lot 1, Glanford using the surname Smoke. Smoak was used for Jacob in an article in Volume 8 of Wentworth Bygones, pp. 66-68 titled Crown Patentees of Glanford.

Jacob Smuck Born in Pennsylvania in 1764 d. 18 Sep 1836 m. Mary b. 18 Mar 1768 d. 29 Aug 1850. Was Susanna his sister? Jacob Smuck had a daughter named Susan, but she was born in 1805 and married Peter Case. Jacob Smoke was a Davenport Phelps settler [26]

Petition dated 26 Jan 1820 [27].
The Petition of Jacob Lewis Smith of the Township of Glanford, District of Gore, Yeoman ... That your Petitioner was born in the State of New Jersey, brought by his parents when an infant to the Province and has been a constant and Loyal Inhabitant thereof for upwards of 31 years. Your Petitioner on 17 Dec 1819 purchased from John Hartford of Township Glanford... Lot 2 Con 1 Glanford, 188 acres (of which 70 being cleared by said Harford) for $1000.00... Said John Hartford has also rendered unto him his Power of Attorney for the purpose of his obtaining a Government Grant Deed forsaid Lot, the same not having been applied for by Hartford, but only located under Davenport Phelps, Esquire, who (it is presumed) had a Grant of said Township from Government 20 years past and upwards.

Signatures are: James M'Clary; Solomon Vanerias; Jacob Hagle; John Dessatt; Francis Heartwell; Henry Flannon; Jacob S Heartwell; Abraham Heartwell; Luke Hogle; Jacob Smith Jr; Amos Smith; Christopher Henry; Joseph Wedge; Stephen Kitsen; Christopher Smith; Edmond Smith; Henry Hagle Junior; **Jacob SMUCK**; David Miller; William Vernon?; Henry Smith; Lewis Smith; John French; Jacob Smith Junior; John Smith; John Vandecar; Benjamin Vandecar; Oen Thomas; David Kotnan; Samuel Hannon; Henry Hannon Jun; William Bechtel; Joseph House - Lieut 5th Lincoln Militia; Fredrick Ashbough; Peter Hagle; Henry Hagle Junr; John Binkley [28]; Rus Tunis; William Binkley; ?Cambrogue?; Henry McKay; George Smith; Isaack Horning;

1. John Henry[1] Peer was born Abt. 1760. He married **Susannah Smoke**.

Notes for John Henry Peer:
James Wedge and Susan(nah) Peer who married 1807 Ontario. Susan was born 1785 Ancaster, daughter of John Henry Peer and Susan(nah) Smoke Information on John Henry Peer comes from the Seth Hastings Grant collection which is housed at the New England Historic Genealogical Society and Libary, Newbury Street, Boston in their unpublished manuscript section. Rev Grant sent a questionnaire to every Wedge he could find in US or Canada around 1898. There is a lot of correspondence from William P Wedge of Sheffield, Beverly Twp, Wentworth Co, Ontario (son of James Wedge and Susan Peer) which states that James Wedge came from Philadelphia Pennsylvania to Hamilton 1804 and married 4 Dec 1807 Susan Peer of Anderkoster [sic – should be Ancaster?] Ontario.

Another letter from William P Wedge states James Wedge was born in Philadelphia on 7 May 1780. He died in Sheffield 28 December 1861. He married 7 June 1807 Susan Pear born 4 August 1785 in Canada (Father John Henry Pear; Mother Susan Smoke) [29]

Child of John Peer and Susannah Smoke is:
+ 2   i. Susannah[2] Peer, born 04 Aug 1785 in Ancaster, Ontario; died Aft. 02 Oct 1868 in Beverley Tp, Wentworth Co. Ontario.

Generation No. 2

2. Susannah[2] Peer (John Henry[1]) was born 04 Aug 1785 in Ancaster, Ontario, and died Aft. 02 Oct 1868 in Beverley Tp, Wentworth Co. Ontario. She married **James Wedge** 07 Jun 1807 in Ancaster, Ontario. He was born 21 Jul 1776 in Pennsylvania, and died 25 Dec 1861 in Sheffield, Bevrley Tp, Wentworth Co. Ontario.

Notes for James Wedge:
James Wedge witnessed Jacob Peer's Will. James Wedge is on 1816 assessment roll of Beverly Twp

1861 census Beverly Tp Wentworth Co. Ontario [30]
James Wedge, gentleman, b US 85, married, Log House
Mrs. J. Wedge, b USA, 67

1861 Census James Wedge

Children of Susannah Peer and James Wedge are:

- 3   i.   Aaron[3] Wedge, born 1807.
- 4   ii.   Oliver Wedge, born 1814; died Bef. 1845. He married Robina Stuart 07 Feb 1838 in West Flamborough Tp Ontario.
- 5   iii.   Aaron Wedge, born 1816.
- 6   iv.   Reuben Wedge, born 1816; died 31 Dec 1850. He married Agnes Nancy Riddell 14 Jun 1838 in Beverley Tp Ontario.
- 7   v.   Susan Wedge, born 1818; died 1904 in Galt, Waterloo Co. Ontario. She married (1) Mr. Hall. She married (2) William Grummett.
- 8   vi.   James Wedge, born 1819. He married Manda Everett.
- 9   vii.   William P. Wedge, born 09 Apr 1820 in Sheffield, Wentworth Co Ontario; died 05 Dec 1911 in Mount Clemens, Macomb Co Michigan. He married Mary Elizabeth Babcock 26 Oct 1850 in Sheffield, Wentworth Co Ontario.
- 10   viii.   Lovina Wedge, born 26 Jun 1820 in Beverley Tp Ontario; died 06 Mar 1896 in Blenheim Twp, Oxford Co, Ontario. She married Joel Smith 28 Jul 1840 in Beverley Tp Ontario.
- + 11   ix.   Wesley Wedge, born 30 Jun 1824 in Beverley Tp Ontario; died Bet. 11 Sep 1854 - 1874 in Beverley Tp Ontario.
- 12   x.   Mary Wedge. She married Thomas Fleming.

Maps

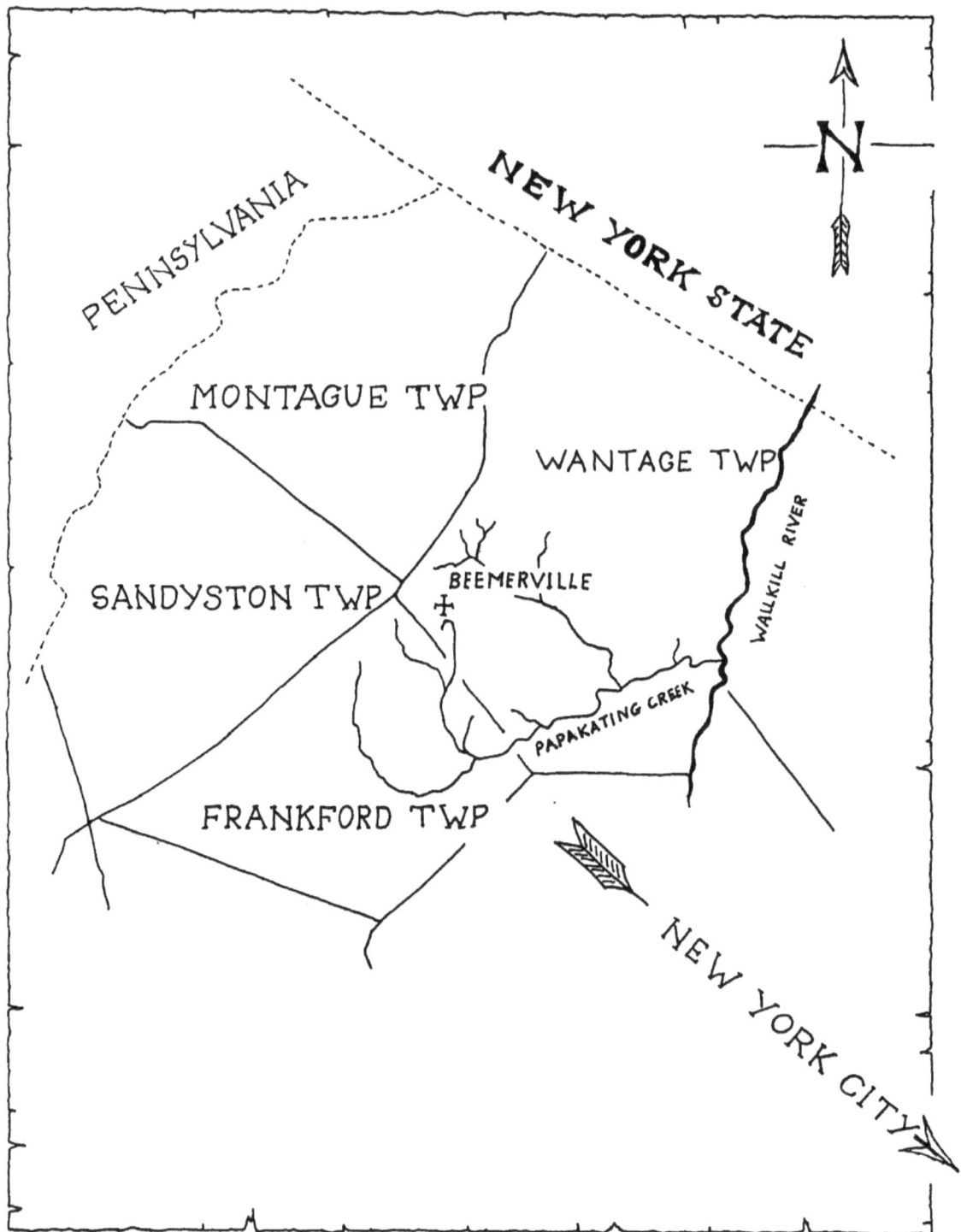

New Jersey showing Papakating Creek. Map by Brian L. Massey

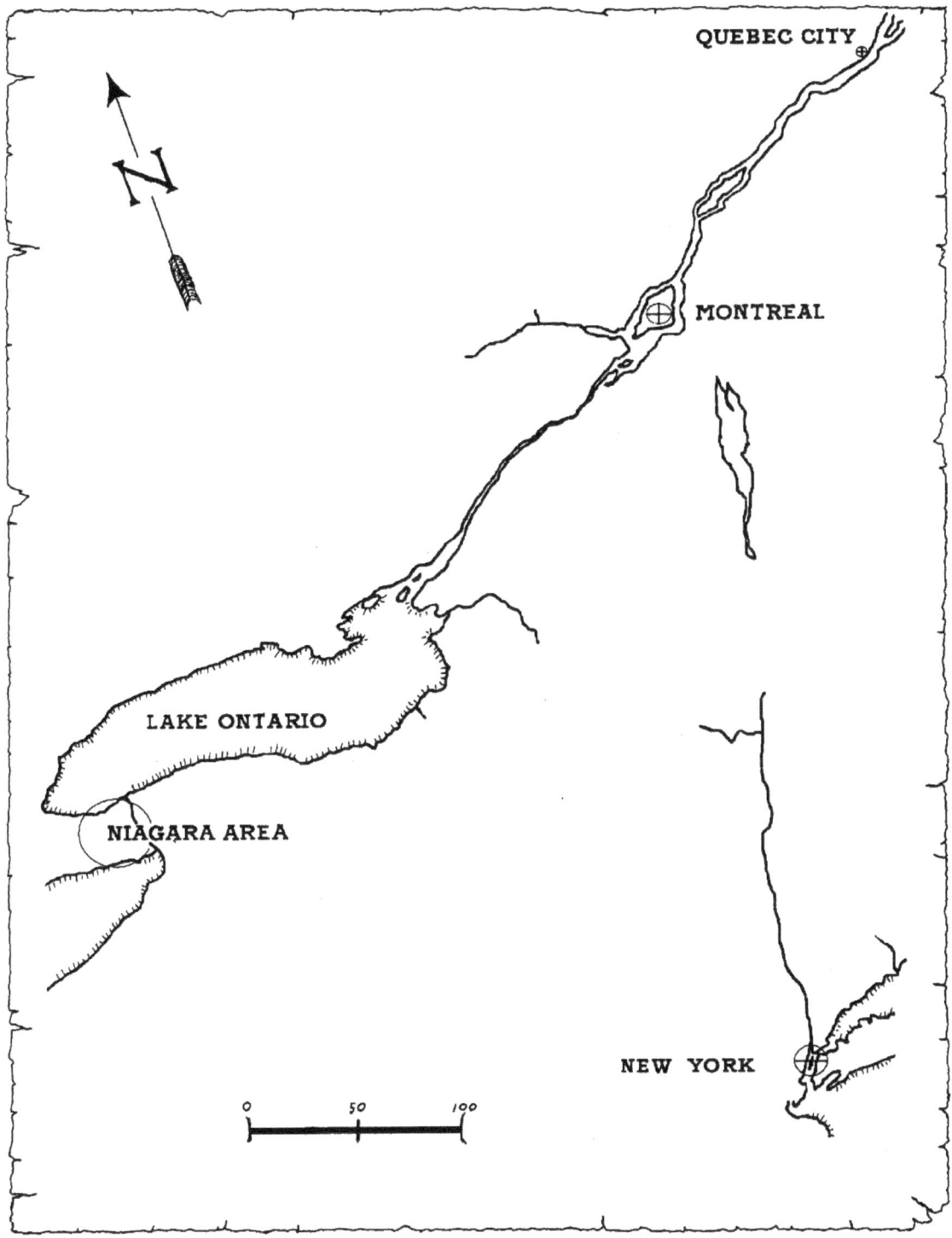

New York & Niagara Area of Upper Canada. Map by Brian L. Massey

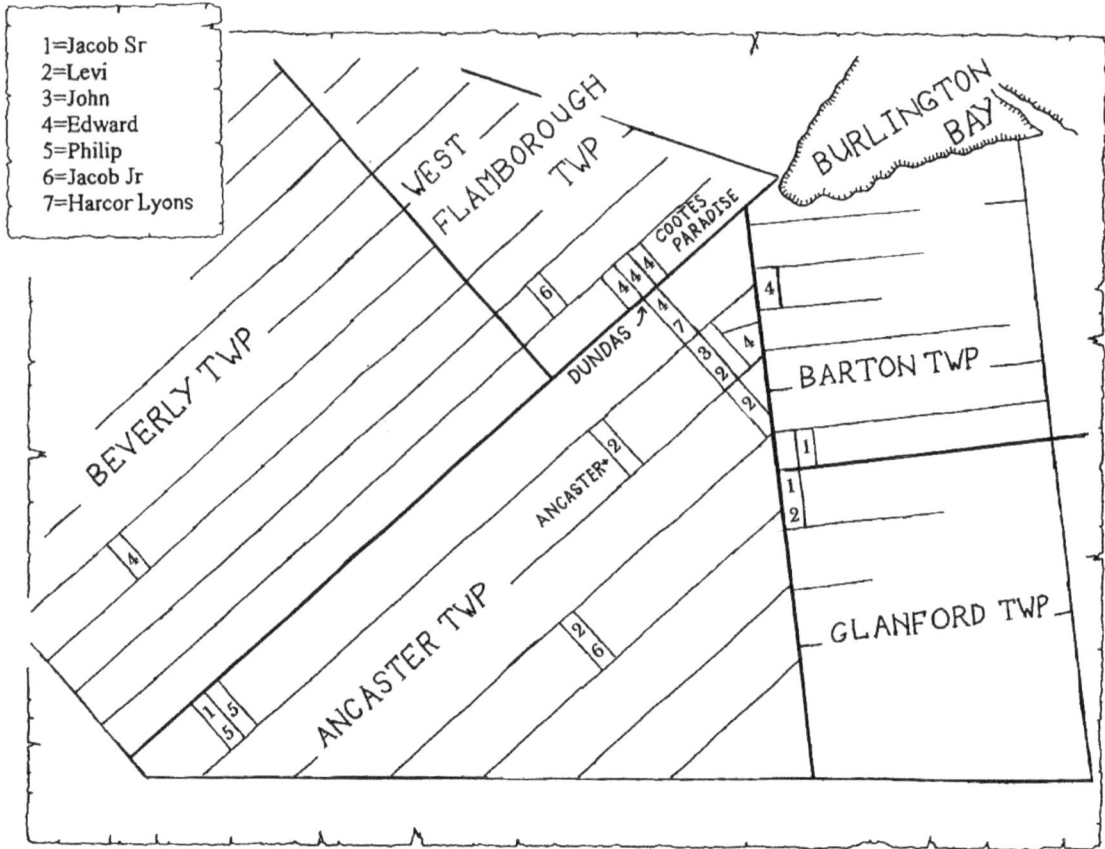

Legend:
1=Jacob Sr
2=Levi
3=John
4=Edward
5=Philip
6=Jacob Jr
7=Harcor Lyons

Lands owned by Peer males in Wentworth County, Upper Canada. Map by Brian L. Massey

Documents for Jacob Peer

Left side of Land Book with entries for the 1797 Land Grants for John, Edward, Philip & Jacob Peer

Right side of Land Book with entries for the 1797 Land Grants for John, Edward, Philip & Jacob Peer

Petition for Land. Niagara 13 July 1797. C2489 3/70 The Petition of Jacob Peer – Humbly Shews – That your Petitioner came to this Province in June 1796 and has a wife and daughter now in Barton where he purchased a farm......Signs with his mark (X)

Affidaviat from Nathaniel Pettit 14 July 1797. C2489 3/70

I do hereby ceritfy that I was acquainted with the bearer Jacob Pear [sic] in the now State of New Jersey and since he came to this province and that he was esteemed on/an – of his --

- --- and much attached to the British Constitution on account of which he suffered greatly both in his person and property in the Late War between Great Britain and America. Certified by Nathl Pettit.

Oath of Allegiance taken by Jacob Peer 13 July 1797. C2489 3/70

I do hereby certify that Jacob Peer Senior appeared before me William Dickson Esquire, -- of his Majesty's -- of the -- in and for the Home District and took the Oath of Allegiance and signed the Declararation this 13th day of July 1797. Signed William Dickson JP

Note: We know that this document says "Senior" rather than "Junior" by a comparison of letter formations. Please note the formation of the upper case letter "J" in "July" and compare it to the formation of the first letter of "Senior" Then compare the first upper case letter of "Signed" (ignore the representation of the & sign which joins with the word "Signed") and you will see that it is identical to the first letter of "Senior"

| Peer Senior | &Signed | July |

38

GRANT to *Jacob Peer*

of the Township of *Barton*

In the County of *Lincoln*

In the _____ District *of Niagara, Yeoman*

all that parcel of Land

In the Township of *Ancaster*

In the County of *Lincoln*

In the _____ District *of Niagara* _____ being

Lot number *5* _____

In the _____ Conceſſion ~~That is to ſay~~

on Dundas Street

commencing in front of the ſaid _____ Conceſſion

At the North Eaſt Angle of _____ — the ſaid Lot

Then South *13* Degrees _____ Minutes Eaſt *100* Chains ~~Links~~
more or leſs, to the allowances for road in rear of the ſaid Conceſſion

Then South *77* Degrees _____ Minutes Weſt *20* Chains ~~Links~~

Then North *13* Degrees _____ Minutes Weſt *100* Chains ~~Links~~
more or leſs, to the front of the ſaid Conceſſion

Then North *77* Degrees _____ Minutes Eaſt *20* Chains ~~Links~~

To the place of beginning

containing *200* Acres _____ more or leſs

For which an allotment of *28* Acres and *4* ſevenths
as ſpecial Specification Lot _____

is made for a Proteſtant Clergy, ~~in lot No.~~ _____ ~~in the~~

~~Conceſſion~~ of the ſaid Township of *Ancaster*

Order in Council *14 July 1797.* D. W. SMITH, Surveyor Gen. U. C.

Warrant No. *1871* S. G. O. fer No.

R. G. O. No. Deſcription Number *10267.*

G. O. No.

A. G. O. No. *3303*

WILL of Jacob Peer

Affidavit, pages 1 & 2

Upper Canada

Surrogate Court } Before Robert Kerr Esquire
Ancaster 6th June 1815 } Judge of said Court

Personally came and appeared this day in open Court William Rymal and Jacob Peer Executors of the Last Will and Testament of Jacob Peer late of Barton deceased, and informed the Court that the said Jacob Peer never was possessed of Lot No thirty seven in the fourth Concession of the Township of Ancaster, but that the said deceased was possessed of Lot Number Thirty eight in the fourth Concession of the said Township of Ancaster, and the said Executors are fully convinced that the said Lot No thirty eight was the Lot intended to be devised to Levi Peer in the Will of the said Jacob Peer deceased, which bears date the ~~twenty~~ Ninth day of January

in the Year of our Lord One thousand
Eight Hundred and two, therefore Know
Ye, that I Robert Kerr Judge as aforesaid
Do hereby decree, that the said Levi
Peer is the true & lawful owner of all
&Singular the said Lot No thirty eight
in the fourth Concession of the said
Township of Ancaster aforesaid, And that
the Executors within mentioned, do give
the said Levi Peer a deed for the Same
In testimony Whereof I have hereunto caused
the Seal of said Court Signed
to be hereunto affixed
Signed
J H Bruck
D Register

R Kerr Judge
S. C

Will & ...

Proved 21st January
1815

...

Robert Rhea
and Surrogate for the
District of ...

Upper Canada

District
of
Niagara

Personally came and appeared before
me Robert Kerr Esquire Surrogate for the
District aforesaid Jasper ... Wyckman of
Augusta in the District aforesaid Esquire
who being duly Sworn on Oath, deposeth
and saith that he was personally
present, when the within mentioned
Testator Jacob Beer Kuins, signed, sealed
& published, pronounced and declared the within
Instrument of writing to be his last Will and Testament
and that David Kerr and James Hodge of Butlers
were also severally present and subscribed with the
... as Witnesses in presence of the said
Testator and of each other, and further this
Deponent saith not.

Jasper ... ...

Sworn before me in Office
... ... the 21st day
of ... 1815

"I, Jacob Peer of the Township of Barton in County of Lincoln and Province of Upper Canada, Senior Husbandman... Considering the great uncertainty of This Mortal life and that it is appointed unto all men once to die and being weak in body, but of sound and disposing mind and memory blessed be Almighty God for the same, do make and Publish this my last Will and Testament, in manner and form following.

That is to say, Firstly, I give and bequeath unto **my son Philip Peer** the sum of one Hundred £ Currency of New York to be paid him by Executors herin after named one year after **my wife Anne** decease & I do also give and Devise to **my son Levi Peer** one Hundred Acres of land being lot Number Thirty seven in the fourth Concession of Ancaster. I do also give and Devise unto **my Daughter Phoebe Mcqueen** Fifty £ Currency of New York to be paid in like manner after the decease of my wife Anne. I also give and Devise unto **my Daughter Marcy Lyon** the sum of Fifty £ like Currency to be paid her the time and in the manner last before mentioned. I do also give and bequeath unto **my son Stephen Peer**, the sum of one Hundred £ New York Currency, to be paid him at ... [continued next page]

53

... the time and manner herin specified.after the decease of my wife Anne. I also give and Devise unto **my Daughter Marcy Lyon** the sum of Fifty £ like Currecnty to be paid her the time and in the manner last before mentioned. I do also give and bequeath unto **my son Stephen Peer**, the sum of one Hundred £ New York Currency, to be paid him at the time and manner herin specified.

I also give and Devise unto **my GrandSons**, the issue of and sons of my son Philip, that is to say, **John Peer, Lewis Peer, Dennis Peer, and Jacob Peer** unto them. Jointly and ...ally [equally?] to be Divided equal between them, all that lot No. 16 in the 7th Concession in the township of Glanford and again I order and devise and also give and bequeath unto wife Anne Peer all and every part of my moveable estate the interest of my money, the rents and incomes of all my real and personal estate and in particular the farm on which I now live being lot number 20 in the 8 concession of the Township of Bar.... [Barton] during her natural lifetime and arther and lastly I devise afer the Decease of my beloved wife Anne that my said farm in Barton the said lot number 20 shall be sold by my said herafter mentioned executors and I also Devise that my personal estate whatsoever my said wife may die in possession of shall also be sold in like manner, farther and lastly my will is that, the residue and remainder of all my estate both real and personal not herin before mentioned and comprises shall be divided and given by my said executors ...

54

... to my said several Sons and Daughters in equal shares and lastly I do appoint **my said son Jacob Peer Jr.** and my trusty friend William Raymal Executors of this my last will and Testament hereby revoking all former wills by me made. In testimony whereof I have herunto set my hand and seal this 29th day of Janua.. [page torn, probably January] of our Lord one Thousand Eight Hundred and Ten.

Signed with an X for Jacob Peer. Witnesses: Samuel Ryckman, David Kern, James Wedge.

An affidavit signed by Jacob Peer Jr and William Rymal stated that Jacob Sr was in error in assigning Lot 37 Concession 4 Ancaster to his son Levi, and it should have read Lot 38, Concession 4. The courts accepted this on 8 June 1815, and granted the land to Levi.

Memorial of Christian Almas dated 3 April 1821 re deed of land Lot 20, Concession 8, Barton Township, belonging to Jacob Peer Sr, deceased. Witness Harcar Lyons. They Land is sold for 248 £ 15s to Jacob Rymal Jr. by Jacob Peer Jr & William Rymal as executors of estate of Jacob Peer Sr. They swear that the original deed from Christian to Jacob Sr was lost or destroyed "during the last war with the United States" (War of 1812)

part compared ... along the ... thereof ... Beginning at a ... from ... of said ... marked ... then North ... two degrees West Twenty Chains, then South Eighteen Degrees West Fifty Chains, then South Seventy Two degrees East Twenty Chains, then North Eighteen Degrees East Fifty Chains, to the plan of beginning, together with all ... out houses ... thereon erected lying and being, and all and singular the hereditaments and appurtenances to the ... belonging or in any wise belonging and their revenues and reversions Remainder and Remainders ... and profits thereof and all the Estate Right Title Interest claim property and demands what soever within at law or in equity of as the said Christian Almas and William Rymal and hereto ... Executors or aforesaid of ... of the same and every part thereof, To have and to hold the same with the Appurtenances, freed and discharged from all incumbrances whatsoever unto the said Jacob Rymal and his heirs and assigns to the sole and proper use, benefit and behoof of the said Jacob Rymal hunies his heirs and assigns for ever under the reservations limitations and conditions expressed in the original grant from the Crown, and that the said Christian Almas, and William Rymal and said Bee do covenant Grant & agree to and with the said Jacob Rymal hunies his heirs and assigns that he the said Jacob Rymal & his heirs and assigns shall and may from time to time and at all times hereafter for ever peaceably and quietly enter into have hold occupy possess and enjoy all and singular the land premises above mentioned and every part and parcel thereof with the appurtenances, without the let trouble hindrance molestation interruption or denial of as the said Christian Almas William Rymal and said Bee for or out heirs or assigns or any other person or persons whatsoever claiming or to claim by from or under or in trust of ... aforesaid and further that the said Christian Almas and William Rymal and said Bee and every of them and ... all and every other person or persons, and his and their heirs having or claiming any Estate Right Title ... or Interest of in or to the said premises above mentioned or any part thereof by from or under or in any ... or others ..., shall and will at all times hereafter upon the reasonable request and at the proper cost & charges of the said Jacob Rymal hunies his heirs and assigns, make do and execute or cause or procure to be made done and executed all and every such further and other lawful and reasonable act or acts thing ... conveyances and assurances in the law whatsoever, for the further better and more perfect granting conveying and assuring of all and singular the ... premises above mentioned with the appurtenances unto the said Jacob Rymal & his heirs or assigns All by the said Jacob Rymal or his heirs or assigns his or their counsel ... shall be lawfully devised advised or required In Witness whereof ... hands and seals ... shall this day and year first above written. And said ...

Margaret Lyons   Jacob Rymal

Documents for John Peer

The Petition of John Peer Humbly Sheweth, that Your Petitioner was a Minor at the time of Warfare between America and Great Britain, but the firm attachment of his Family to His Majesty, hopes will suffice to remove all doubts – to his Loyalty. Your Petitioner begs leave to refer your Excellency to Nathaniel Pettit Esquire's Certificate. Your Petitioner married the Widow of Thomas Millard Jr, her former husband served in Col. Butler's Rangers. Your Petitioner prays a Grant of 200 acres for himself and likewise a further grant for his wife and the lands of her deceased husband for the use of his heir and your Petitioner will every pray. John Peer. Newark July 1795.

--- Certify that I was acquainted with the Bearer John Pere and the young in the Time of the War between Great Britain and American had little to do in it but was of a familywho was well and firmly attached to the Crown and Constitution of Britain and Since that hath supported the Character of an honest Industrious man. Certified by Nathl. Pettit. Newark July 16th 1795

4 July 1796. John Peer. Recommended for 200 acres for himself if not granted before, but it does not appear that his wife has been the daughter of a U. E. Loyalist. Source: Upper Canada Land Book B 1794-1797. C101

His Honor Peter Rupsell Esquire President of the Government of Upper Canada etc etc In Council

The Petition of John Peer of Ancaster Humbly Shews

That your Petitioner has been nine years in the Province and has a family that he has never received any Certificate or Order in Council for Land – Therefore humbly prays your Honor would be pleased to confirm a grant of two hundred acres

And as in Duty bound your Petitioner will every Pray

John Peer

Niagara

13 July 1797

Ancaster, December 18th 1798

Mr. Smith

Sir

I have the goodness to present Malon Bray the Bearer hereof to locate 200 acres of land for me. The Warrant for the same Mr. Dixon left at your office. Which he was to locate but had not the Distance and season of the year makes it difficult for me to come in person

I am your most
Humble Servant
John Peer

Mr. Smith

1808 (P)
9 February 1808
Bond

Levi Peer
Richard Hatt Esq
Edward Peer
And
Stephen Peer

Estate of John Peer

Conrad Felman
David Kern
Appraisers

Know all men by these presents that we Levi Peer
Richard Hatt Edward Peer and Stephen Peer ——

———————————— all of the County of Lincoln: In
District of Niagara Province of Upper Canada are held and
firmly bound to the Governor, Lieutenant Governor or Person
Administering the Government of the said Province, in the
Sum of One Thousand Pounds, of good and lawful money
of this Province. To be well and truly Paid to the said Governors Lieut Governors or Person Administering the Government
for the time being and for which Payment So to be made
WE bind ourselves, Our Heirs, Executors and Administrators
firmly by these Presents Sealed with our Seals and dated
at Niagara this Ninth day of February, in the Year of
Our Lord One thousand Eight Hundred & Eight,

THE Condition of this Obligation is such
that, if the above bounden Levi Peer Richard Hatt Edward
Peer and Stephen Peer ——————————————

Administrators ——————— of all and the Goods, Chattels,
and Credits of John Peer —————————— deceased Do make
or cause to be made a true and perfect Inventory of all and
Singular the Goods, Chattels, and Credits of the said
John Peer ——————————— deceased which shall have come
to the hands possession or knowledge of the said Levi Peer
Richard Hatt Edward Peer and Stephen Peer ————

—————————————————— or into the Hands of any
other Person or Persons, for the said Levi Peer Richard Hatt

Edward Peer and Stephen Peer — — — —

— — — — — — — or either of them, and the same

so made do exhibit or cause to be exhibited into the Office of the

Surrogate of the District of Niagara at or before the expiration

of Six Calendar Months from the date of the above mentioned

Obligation and the same goods Chattles & Credits of the said

deceased at the time of his death which at any time after

that come to the hands and possession of the said Levi Peer

Richard Hatt Edward Peer and Stephen Peer

or into the hands and possession of any other person or persons for the

said Levi Peer Richard Hatt Edward Peer and Stephen

Peer — — — — Then this Obligation to be void and of none

effect or else to remain in full force and virtue —

Signed and   Levi Peer
Sealed in
Presence of us

Robert Kerr

                    Edward Peer

                    Stephen Peer

Know all men by these present? That we Levi Peer, Richard Hatt, Edward Peer and Stephen Peer all of the County of Lincoln District of Niagara Province of Upper Canada are held and firmly bound to the Governors Lieutenant Governor or Person Administering the Government of the said Province in the Sum of One Thousand £ of Good and Lawful Money, of this Province to be well and truly Paid to the said Governors Lieut. Governors or Person Administering the Government for the time being and for which Payment so to be made we bind ourselves, our heirs, Executors and Administrators firmly by these present Sealed with our Seals and dated at Niagara this Nineth day of February in the Year of our Lord One Thousand Eight Hundred & Eight.

The Condition of this Obligation is such that if the above bound Levi Peer, Richard Hatt, Edward Peer and Stephen Peer, Administrators, of all and the Goods, Chattles and Credits of John Peer, deceased, do make or cause to be made a true and perfect Inventory of all and singular the goods, chattles and credits of the said John Peer, deceased, which shall have come to the hands & possession or knowledge of the said Levi Peer, Richard Hatt, Edward Peer and Stephen Peer, or into the hands of any other Person or Persons for the said Levi Peer, Richard Hatt, Edward Peer and Stephen Peer, or either of them so made do exhibit or cause to be exhibited into the office of the Surrogate of the District of Niagara at or before the expiration of Six Calendar months from the date of the above written Obligation and the same goods, Chattles and Credits of the asid deceased at the time of his death which at any time after shall come into the hands and possession of the said Levi Peer, Richard Hatt, Edward Peer and Stephen Peer, or into the hands and possession of any other peros or persons for the said Levi Peer, Richard Hatt, Edward Peer and Stephen Peer, then the Obligation to be void and of none effect or else to remain in full force and virtue.

Signed Levi Peer, Edward Peer, Stephen Peer
Signed and sealed Robert Kerr, --- Smith

We Levi Peer of Glanford and Richard Hatt of Ancaster, in the County of Lincoln, Province of Upper Canada, do swear, that we will firmly and truly administer all and singular, the goods and chattels, rights and credits of John Peer, late of Ancaster, deceased, and pay all his debts and Legacies as far as his Estate will extend, and the law? Change, and that w will a true inventory make of the rights and credits, goods and chattels, and effects of the said john Peer, deceased, and exhibit the same, ---

Appraisers, as may be appointed, to apriase and value the same, and that we will with all convenient speed, the said inventory, together with the said appraisement, certified under [crease in paper obscures this part in copy but it reads "under the hands of the"] the appraiser – unto the office of the Surrogate Court, for this District. And we do further swear that we do not know the said John Peer, deceased, left any Last Will or Testament, in writing or otherwise, and that we do believe he died intestate. So help us God. (signed) Levi Peer

Niagara Surrogate Office 9th February 1808

To Robert Kerr, Esquire, Judge of the Surrogate Court for the District of Niagara.

The Petition of Livi Pierre [sic]
Humbly Sheweth

That John Pierre [sic] your Petitioners Brother, died as your Petitioner vierily believes, without a last Will and Testament, Your Petioner being the oldest Brother & next of Kin to the deceased, Humbly prays that Letters of Administration may be granted him to Sell the Estate of said John Pierre [sic], deceased.
And your Petioner as in duty bound will ever pray

(Signed) Levi Peer

Niagara, the 9th day of February 1808

Inventory of the Goods, Chattels and Credits of the late John Peer, taken the 13th of February 1808

Inventory taken by Levi Peer & Rich.d Hatt Administrator of the Estate of the John Peer Deceased & appraised as & Warrant to Conrad Fellman & David Keer 13th February 1808 —

Item	£	s	d
1 Horse Colt ab.t 3 Yrs old	16		
1 Bay Horse 7 ..	21		
1 Grey Mare	21		
1 Sled Horse Harness for 2 Horses Com.t	4		
1 Cutg Box Knife &c complete		12	
1 Dung Fork & Pitchfork		10	
1 Scoop Shovel & Empty barrel		12	
1 Box		1	
1 piece of a Chair		11	
1 Iron & Harrow pegs	2	17	
1 wood Sleigh	1	12	
1 Cow	6		
1 Plough & Irons with Clevis	2	8	
1 Harrow with 9 Iron teeth	2	4	
3 Hoggs after fatting	6		
1 Iron of Bees		8	
1 Grindstone	1	6	
		8	

Item	£	s	d
1 Barrel about half full of Beef	1		
2 Barrels with flour & 1 D.t ab.t 3/4 full	2	10	
1 Barr.l & Sugatub & Bakertray		8	
2 Iron Brushes & some soap fat	1	4	
Walnut Scantling for 4 Bed Steads		12	
1 Little Wheel	1	4	
Some wool & a Keg		4	
1 Turning Lathe		10	
9 Walnut Boards		6	
2 Barrels & some Crout		4	
Some Potatoes about 2 Bush.l		6	
3 Bush.l Potatoes buried		9	
1 Box of Paint		2	
1 Rifle Powder Horn & Shot bag	6		
Some dryed Beef		8	
1 pr Hand Irons, Shovel & tongs	2		
1 Tea Kittle	1		
8 Old Chairs	1	4	
1 Spade		8	
1 Iron Pot		15	
2 Trammels		4	
1 Wash Tub		6	
1 Iron bound Keg		2	
1 Frying pan 4/ Knot bowl 2/		6	

1 horse colt abt 3 years old	2 pr cakes of Tallow
1 Bay horse	1 Walnut Table with Candles in drawer
1 Gray Mare	1 Bucket 2/ 1 Maul & Rings? 5/
1 set Horse Harness for 2 horses complete	1 Pump Auger & Ta—Bit
1 Cu—Box Knife – complete	1 bake Oven & Bail? 12/ Iron Pot 24/
1 Dung? Fork & Pitchfork	1 Saddle & Bridle
1 Scoop Shovel & Empty barrel	1 Keglor & Bra—Hoe
1 box	1 Small walnut chest
1 piece of a chain	5 Hives & 1 Ba—
1 S—H-- --	1 Adze, Broad Axe & Hand Axe
1 Wood Sleigh	4 Augers
1 C—	4 Planes
1 Plough & Irons with _ivis	1 Plough & Gr—
1 Harrow with 9 –	1 Axe & 1 Chest of Tools
3 Hogs in a pen fatting	1 Skimmer & Beef Fork
1 Hive of Bees	1 Copping Axe & Conk Shell
1 Grinder –	1 – Trowel & Graining Knife
1 Soap Tub Bucket & K—ler	Cauldron
1 barrel about half full of Beef	BedStead -- & Bed –

2 Barrel with flour & 1 do? [ditto?] – Salt	1 ox bell & hand saw?
1 Barrel 1 Deye? Tub & 1 B—of Hay	Crockery Wine Glasses
2 Work Benches & Some Soap, --	Tumblers & Decanturs
Walnut Scandling? for 4 Bedsteads	1 earthen Jug
1 Little Wheel	2 Pewter Basins & Pewter Plates & Knives
Some Wool & a Keg	& forks
1 Turning Lathe	Spoons -- & E-- & Be—complete
9 Walnut boards	1 coat & 2 flannel shirts
2 Barrels & some Crout?	2 pr Coveralls & Shirt Jacket
Some potatoes about 2 bushels	4 Waistcoats & 2 muslin Shirts
2 Bushels Potatoes, burried	2 pr socks
1 Box of paint	1 hat
1 Rifle, Powder Horn & Shot Bag	1 auger
Some Dryed Beef	1 small Stack—Wheat
1 pr Hand Irons, Shovel & Tongs	Wheat in the barn
1 Tea Kettle	Part of a stack of Hay
8 old Chains	Wheat Ground & Wheat Sowing
1 Spade	Rye (ditto)
1 Iron Pot	Rye in the barn
2 Trammels?	Bus—Shares & I. Skinners
1 Wash Tub	John Smiths note
1 Iron Bound Keg	Balance on P. Jordon's ditto [note]
1 Frying Pan 4/. Knot bowl 2/	Serviss's –
2 Flat Irons	Henry Millers Note
1 Knot E—	Wm Killman's note
1 pr wool cards	Balance on Bar—Sweet's note
1 Flax Seed Veine	J—Leodys? –
1 pr small Halyards	Andrew Tunf—ditto
1 Churn, some pork in it	Miller? Laurason –
1 Green? with dryed Apples	Henry Young
1 Bible, 3 Books & Employ—	M. McMullins –
1 Basket	David Newtons –
1 Keg about half full white lead	E—m Smith
1 Crock & some Honey	Jacob Smoak
1 SexthSmith & Ring? & Wedges	Jonathan Omstead
1 Nail Box with Sundries in it	W. Tonger

The final tally of Credits and Debts was 209£ 7 s 5 p

Grandchildren of Jacob & Anna Peer

For full details of children and grandchildren of Jacob and Anna please refer to the volumes on each son and daughter of Jacob and Anna. Each volume will include footnoted sources, copies of documents such as land records, land petitions, census, etc., as well as newspaper clippings, letters, family photographs and other miscellaneous items.

CHILDREN OF LEVI PEER & ELIZABETH MARICAL

i. **possibly an unknown daughter Peer** was born between 1794-1804.

ii. **Levi Peer** was born in Feb 1807 in Wellington Co. Ontario. He married Jane Greenlees on 12 May 1836. He died on 15 Aug 1895 in Guelph, Wellington Co. Ontario.

iii. **William Marrical Peer** was born about 1810 in Ontario. He married Martha after 1859. He died on 10 Oct 1878 in Grover Tp, Wayne Co. South Wayne City Illinois.

iv. **Abraham Peer** was born on 16 Apr 1813 in Ancaster, Ontario or New York. He married Mary Ann Burton on 12 Oct 1837 in Hamilton Co. Illinois. He died on 17 Mar 1879 in Crouch Tp., Hamilton Co. Illinois.

v. **Rachel Peer** was born about 1818 in Pennsylvania. She married Levi (Lee) Lewis Hall on 16 Nov 1839 in Hamilton Co. Illinois. She died after 1860.

vi. **Hiram Peer** was born on 12 Apr 1821 in Pennsylvania or Ontario. He married Kitsey Jane (Betsy) Hall on 04 Feb 1844. He died on 13 Jan 1852 in Big Mound Tp., Wayne Co., Illinois.

vii. **Eliza Jane Peer** was born on 09 Jan 1824 in Pennsylvania. She married James Relaford Hall on 04 Dec 1844 in Hamilton Co. Illinois. She died on 08 Jul 1902 in Hamilton Co. Illinois.

CHILDREN OF EDWARD & ANNA PEER

i. **John L. Peer** was born about 1792 in Canada West. He married Nancy Harris before 1817. He died on 29 Aug 1852 in Jerseyville, Ancaster Tp. Ontario.

ii. **Jacob Peer** was born on 26 Jan 1796 in Canada. He married Amanda Loomis before 1819. He died on 25 Mar 1885 in Gavin, Oklahoma.

iii. **Mercy (aka Phoebe) Peer** was born between 1800-1802 in Canada. She married Stephen Averill before 1819. She died between 1860-1870 in Pennsylvania.

iv. **Lewis A. Peer** was born on 02 Feb 1802 in Upper Canada. He married Charlotte before 1825 in Northeast Tp., Erie Co. PA. He died on 08 Nov 1891 in Northeast Tp., Erie Co. PA .

CHILDREN OF EDWARD & SARAH PEER

i. **Barzilla King Peer** was born about 30 Apr 1813 in Canada. He married Nancy Prudence Hale on 01 May 1853 in Berrien Co. Michigan. He died on 13 Dec 1877 in Bertrand, Berrien Co, Michigan.

CHILDREN OF PHILIP PEER AND ESTHER DUNN

i. **Alphaeus (Aaron or Alfred) Peer**, born Bet. 1792 - 1797 in Upper Canada; died Aft. 1841. He married (1) Mary Ann Young 30 Apr 1829 in Nassagaweya Tp. Halton Co. Ontario born Abt. 1800 possibly in Canajoharie New York; died 21 May 1842 in Ontario. He married (2) Catherine Greenfield Aft. 1842.

ii. **Mary Pear**, born Abt. 1797 in Ontario or Pennsylvania, USA; died 19 Apr 1888 in Nassagewaya, Halton Co. Ontario. She married Simon DeForest 16 Jun 1819 in Halton Co. Ontario; born 05 Mar 1789 in Upper Canada; died 12 Sep 1861 in Halton Co. Ontario.

iii. **John Peer**, born Bet. 1797 - 1800 in Ontario or Pennsylvania; died 21 Aug 1888 in Toronto, Ontario. He married Mary Ann Oliphant 1829; born Abt. 1802 in Wentworth Co. Ontario; died 07 Jan 1887 in Toronto, Peel Co. Ontario.

iv. **Jacob Peer**, born Abt. 1804 in Canada; died Aft. 1880 in Michigan. He married Mary Corner Bef. 1826; born 18 Jun 1809 in New York; died in Michigan.

v. **Dennis Peer**, born 17 Jul 1804 in Ancaster Ontario; died 19 Oct 1881 in Cainsville, Ontario. He married Catherine Mullen 25 May 1827; born 12 Sep 1804 in Onondago, Ontario; died 25 Sep 1898 in Cainsville, Ontario.

vi. **Lewis Peer**, born Bef. 1810 in Canada.

CHILDREN OF PHILIP PEER AND SUSAN GRINIAUS

i. **Jane Peer**, born 26 Dec 1815 in possibly Erin Tp. Wellington Co. Ontario; died 09 Jul 1907 in Erin Tp., Wellington Co. Ontario. She married Isaac Dingman Bef. 1833 in Ontario; born Bet. 03 Feb 1800 - 1804 in Upper Canada; died Aft. 1881 in probably Wellington Co. Ontario.

ii. **Philip Peer**, born 29 Jan 1819 in Ontario; died 14 Feb 1904 in Anabel Tp Bruce Co. Ontario. He married (1) Charity Lampman Bef. 1846 in Ancaster, Wentworth Co. Ontario; born 01 Oct 1825 in Ancaster, Wentworth Co. Ontario; died 25 Dec 1862 in

Puslinch Tp. Wellington Co. Ontario. He married (2) Janet Forsyth 17 Jan 1867 in Ancaster, Ontario; died 05 Jul 1928 in Yorkton, Saskatchewan.

iii. **Ruth Peer**, born 02 Apr 1821 in Halton Co. Ontario or Pennsylvania; died 13 Oct 1871 in Mountsberg, E. Flamborough Tp. Ontario. She married James Hurren; born 12 Nov 1809 in Linstead Parva, Suffolk Eng

CHILDREN OF JACOB PEER & LUCY POWERS

i. **Lydia Peer** was born about 1798. She married Amasa Hemenger on 01 May 1843 in St. Clair Co. MI.

ii. **Euphemia B. Peer** was born in 1802. She married Andrew Hull Westbrook about 1820 in MI. She died on 07 Jul 1870 in Marine City, St. Clair Co. Michigan.

iii. **Violetta Peer** was born on 05 Oct 1804 in Ontario. She married Ebenezer Westbrook on 16 Dec 1823 in St. Clair Co. Michigan. She died on 11 Aug 1864 in Michigan.

iv. **Lucretia Peer** was born about 1808 in Ontario. She died after 1870 in Algonac, Michigan.

v. **James L. Peer** was born about 1810. He died on 26 Nov 1846 in Lake Erie, Ontario.

vi. **Aaron G. Peer** was born on 27 Feb 1812 in Dundas, Ontario. He married Euphemia L. Westbrook on 27 Jan 1841 in China Tp. St. Clair Co. MI. He died on 22 Oct 1891 in Algonac, Michigan.

vii. **Jacob Peer** was born on 17 Dec 1814 in Ontario. He married Maria Eastwood on 21 Dec 1853 in Clay Tp. St. Clair Co. MI. He died on 02 Jun 1893 in Algonac, Michigan.

viii. **Lucy Peer** was born on 17 Dec 1814 in Dundas, Ontario. She married Aura P. Stewart on 26 Jul 1856 in St. Clair Co. MI. She died on 09 Jan 1897 in Algonac, Michigan.

CHILDREN OF STEPHEN PEER & LYDIA SKINNER

i. **Stephen Peer** was born in Aug 1811 in Stamford, Ontario. He died on 04 Jul 1864 in Markham, Ontario. He married Ann Forster. He died 04 Jul 1864 in Markham Ontario

ii. **Edward Peer** was born on 31 Jul 1814 in Stamford, Welland Co. Ontario. He married Catherine Hagerty before 1840. He died on 15 Mar 1861 in Ontario.

CHILDREN OF PHOEBE PEER & DANIEL MCQUEEN

i. **Nancy McQueen** was born in 1787 in NJ. She married James Simpson McCall on 30 Aug 1807 in Charlotteville, Norfolk Co. Ontario. She died in 1870 in Charlotteville Tp, Norfolk Co. Ontario.

ii. **Sarah McQueen** was born about 1789 in Bertie Tp, Welland Co. Ontario. She died on 29 Mar 1879 in Vittoria, Charlotteville, Norfolk Co. Ontario.

iii. **Abigail McQueen** was born on 15 May 1789 in Fort Erie, Ontario. She married Isaac Smith in 1809 in Flamborough West, Ontario. She died on 16 May 1862 in Ontario.

iv. **Mary McQueen** was born about 1791 in Bertie Tp, Welland Co. Ontario. She died on 17 Oct 1861 in Middleton Tp. Norfolk Co..

v. **James McQueen** was born on 12 May 1794 in Bertie Tp, Welland Co. Ontario. He married Elizabeth Wood in 1820. He died on 11 Dec 1877 in Southwold Heights, Southwold Tp. Elgin Co. Ontario.

vi. **Jacob McQueen** was born about 1798 in Bertie Tp, Welland Co. Ontario.

vii. **Elizabeth (Betsey) McQueen** was born about 1799 in Bertie Tp, Welland Co. Ontario.

viii. **Alexander McQueen** was born about 1802.

ix. **Hannah McQueen** was born on 15 May 1805 in Long Point, Norfolk Co. Ontario. She married David Hall on 28 Jul 1833.

x. **Hugh McQueen** was born about 1807 in Woodhouse Tp, Norfolk Co. Ontario. He died before 03 Nov 1868.

xi. **Daniel McQueen** was born about 1810 in Woodhouse Tp, Norfolk Co. Ontario. He married Caroline Cynthia Bostwick on 17 May 1835.

CHILDREN OF MARCY PEER & HARCOR LYONS

i. **Lewis Lyons** was born on 07 Aug 1793.

ii. **Anne Lyons** was born on 19 Sep 1795. She died on 14 Oct 1867 in Waterdown, Ontario.

iii. **Phoebe Lyons** was born on 12 Jul 1797. She married James Truesdale on 18 Oct 1818. She died on 27 Oct 1839.

iv. **Joseph Lyons** was born on 23 Nov 1798. He died in Apr 1872.

v. **Elizabeth Lyons** was born on 06 Aug 1800. She died on 25 Aug 1847 in Waterdown, Ontario.

vi. **Jane Lyons** was born on 28 Jan 1802. She married Platt Nash on 29 Dec 1830 in Ancaster, Ontario. She died on 19 Jan 1872 in Dundas, Ontario.

vii. **Mary Lyons** was born on 13 Nov 1803 in West Flamborough, Ontario. She died on 24 Dec 1833 in Oakville, Ontario.

viii. **Edward Lyons** was born on 06 Aug 1805 in West Flamborough Tp. Wentworth Co. Ontario. He married Orpha Smith in 1829. He died on 03 Mar 1890 in Dundas, Wentworth Co Ontario.

ix. **Jacob Lyons** was born on 17 Jan 1806. He died on 31 Jul 1815 in West Flamborough Tp. Wentworth Co. Ontario.

x. **John Lyons** was born on 12 Jan 1810. He died on 12 Aug 1827 in West Flamborough Tp. Wentworth Co. Ontario.

xi. **Marcia Lyons** was born on 10 Oct 1812. She died on 15 Oct 1850 in Dundas, Ontario.

xii. **Harcor Lyons** was born on 08 Mar 1814 in Ontario. He married Hannah Cummins on 22 Sep 1838 in West Flamborough Tp. Ontario. He died in Sep 1888 in Algenac, MI, USA.

xiii. **Hannah Lyons** was born on 17 Jul 1815. She died on 17 Feb 1817 in West Flamborough Tp. Wentworth Co. Ontario.

xiv. **Jeremiah Lyons** was born on 13 Nov 1816 in Dundas, Wentworth Co. Ontario. He married Maryann Marical on 03 Mar 1838 in West Flamborough Tp. Ontario. He died on 20 Aug 1895 in Dundas, Ontario.

xv. **Sarah Lyons** was born in 1819. She married Abram Kelly on 18 May 1834. She died on 16 Jan 1860 in Burford, Brant Co. Ontario.

Debunking the Myths

There are so many online trees with bad genealogy and with incorrect linking of one generation to another that it becomes overwhelming to think about trying to provide corrections.

In the case of our Peer family, the two most prevalent are the unsourced claim that our Jacob's wife was Johanna Harriman and the unsourced claim that our Jacob was the son of Johannes (aka John) Peer and Susanna Ruttan. When I talk about an "unsourced claim" I mean an entry for which there is no proof, and no sources have ever been given to support the claim. I wrote an article many years ago stating that "genealogy without sources is mythology". As good genealogists we should never write something as if it were fact when we have no proof of our statement.

UNSOURCED CLAIM #1: JOHANNA HARRIMAN AS OUR JACOB'S WIFE

There was a Johanna Harriman who did marry a Jacob Peer in Rockaway New Jersey. This couple lived their entire lives in Rockaway, Morris County New Jersey. In 1795 they are are shown as being members of Rockaway Parish. Johanna (Harriman) Peer is also shown as having died in Rockaway in 1816.

Since we know that our Jacob arrived in Upper Canada from Sussex County New Jersey in June 1796 and we know that he lived the rest of his life in Upper Canada it is impossible for him to also be living in Rockaway.

As well Johanna (Harriman) Peer died in 1816 in Rockaway but our Jacob's wife Anna died in Upper Canada where she had lived since 1796.

Johanna Harriman and Jacob Peer had known children born in Rockaway. One son, Jacob Jr., was born in Denville, New Jersey, in 1804 as the son of Jacob Peer and Johanna Harriman. He married Hannah Shawger and had a family. He died on 18 Apr 1879 in Rockaway, New Jersey, USA.

All we need do is look at the proven children of our Jacob and Anna. Their children include a son Jacob Jr. born ca 1776 in New Jersey. This Jacob married Lucy Powers and settled in Michigan. It seems clear that Jacob and Joanna Peer did not have two sons both named Jacob, born 28 years apart who lived and married in two different locations.

Notice also the dates of births. Our Jacob and Anna's children were born between ca 1760 and ca 1780. Johanna Harriman is known to have been born in 1771. It is therefore impossible for her to be the woman our Jacob married and the mother of his children.

UNSOURCED CLAIM #2 JOHANNES (JOHN) PEER & SUSANNA RUTTAN AS OUR JACOB'S PARENTS

Johannes (Jan or John) Peer was baptised 04 October 1688 in Belleville, Essex Co. New Jersey. His parents were Teunis Jansen Pier and Catrina Tomasse Cadmus. Johannes (John) married Susanna Ruttan and lived in Rockaway New Jersey.

Their son Jacob Janse Peer (aka Pier) was baptised with his brother Cornelis at the age of 4, on 13 July 1729 in New Jersey. [31] He is not in his father's will probated in July 1760 which may indicate he was no longer living on that date.

Probate of Wills: July 21, 1760: John Peer of Hanover, Morris Co. New Jersey. Wife inherited but not named. Sons Abraham, Daniel, Cornelius, David inherited land. Sons John and Samuel and daughters Catherine and Jean inherited money.

Calendar of Wills, Adminstrations etc. Vol. IV. 1761-1770. 1760 July 21. Peer, John of Hanover Morris Co. will of. To my wife the house and lands where I live and after her death I give my lands to my 4 sons - Abraham, Daniel, Cornelius and David. Son Tunis 27 L. Son John 30 L. son Samuel 20 L. Daughter catherine 30 L. Daughter Jean 30 L. Executors sons Dainel and Cornelius Peer. Witnesses Lewis Stewart, John Parlaman, Proved April 21, 1763. April 27 Inventor L267.5.1 made by George Bowlby and John Parlaman

There is not a shred of evidence to support the claim that our Jacob Peer is this man. What individuals making this claim seem to forget is that there were several men named Jacob Peer in New Jersey at the same time as our Jacob. Simply having the same name does not mean person A is the same individual as person B. This is where the careful researcher will look for proof of their theory, and if they can't find any, they will explain any circumstantial evidence that supports their theory. Without some proof or supporting facts, they are just creating mythology and perpetuating incorrect genealogy.

Other Ontario Peer Families: Peter Peer & Mary Graham

The family of Peter Peer and Mary Gaham appear in Upper Canada in the Leeds County area. They do not appear to be connected to our Peer family but I am including the research I have done on the family for comparison. Please note that I did not conduct intensive or extensive research on this family as it was not my main interest.

Peter Peer. He died before 1851. **Mary Graham** was born about 1792 in Canada. She died after 1861. Peter Peer and Mary Graham married. They had the following children:

i. Peter Peer was born about 1820 in Canada. He died after 1851.

2. ii. Reuben Peer was born on 26 Feb 1820 in Ontario. He died on 26 Feb 1899 in Elizabethtown Twp, Leeds County Ontario[1].

3. iii. Oliver Peer was born on 05 Feb 1821 in Elizabethtown, Leeds Co. Ontario. He died on 04 Sep 1904 in Athens, Leeds Co. Ontario[2].

4. iv. Stephen B. Peer was born about 1824 in Canada. He married Rosanna Tryon on 01 Oct 1845 in Johnstown District Ontario[3]. He died in 1888[4].

7.v. Britann (Ann) Peer was born before 1828.

5.vi. Mary Peer was born about 1829 in Yonge Tp Ontario. She died after 1861.

vii. Charles Metcalf (Metcalf) Peer was born about 1833 in Canada.

6. viii. Hannah Peer was born on 18 Mar 1833 in Addison, Elizabethtown-Kitley Tp, Leeds Co. Ontario[4]. She married Benjamin Scott between 1851-1854 in Ontario. She died on 07 Jun 1908 in Leeds Co. Ontario[5].

ix. John Peer.

Generation 2

2. **Reuben Peer**-2 (Peter-1) was born on 26 Feb 1820 in Ontario. He died on 26 Feb 1899 in Elizabethtown Twp, Leeds County Ontario[1]. **Margaret Keough** was born on 23 Feb 1832 in USA. She died on 29 Apr 1890. Reuben Peer and Margaret Keough married.They had the following children:

i. Reuben Peer was born between 24 Apr 1853-1856 in Brockville, Ontario. He married Florence Mabel Smith on 09 Feb 1887 in Brockville, Leeds Co. Ontario. He died on 20 Dec 1938 in Watertown, New York?.

ii. Mary Lilly Peer was born about 1857 in Ontario.

iii. Hannah Jane Peer was born about 1860 in Ontario. She married Charles Newton Brown on 21 Jan 1890 in Grenville, Ontario.
iv. William James Peer was born about 1860 in Elizabethtown, Leeds County Ontario. He married Wilhelmina (Minnie) Cooper on 07 Jun 1899 in Grenville, Ontario[6]. He died on 02 Apr 1902 in Elizabethtown, Leeds Co. Ontario[7].

v. Lucy Adeline Peer was born on 07 Nov 1866 in Ontario.

vi. Margaret Anne Peer was born about 1868 in Elizabethtown Ontario. She married George Rowsom on 24 May 1899 in Grenville, Ontario.

vii. Katherine Matilda (Katie) Peer was born in Jun 1870 in Ontario. She died in 1940.

viii. Clarissa (Clara) Melvina Peer was born on 02 Sep 1873 in Greenbush, Leeds & Grenville Co. Ontario[8]. She married Milton Lionel Hinton on 05 Apr 1899 in Lanark Co. Ontario[9].

3. **Oliver Peer**-2 (Peter-1) was born on 05 Feb 1821 in Elizabethtown, Leeds Co. Ontario. He died on 04 Sep 1904 in Athens, Leeds Co. Ontario[2]. **Sarah Jane Charters** was born on 10 Sep 1833 in Ireland. She died on 29 Sep 1901 in Ketley Tp, Leeds Co. Ontario[10]. Oliver Peer and Sarah Jane Charters married.They had the following children:

i. Nancy Peer was born about 1854. She married John Forsythe on 12 Aug 1873 in Leeds & Grenville Co. Ontario.

ii. John Albert Peer was born about 1855 in Kitley Ontario. He married Mary Tink on 30 Sep 1879 in New Edinburgh Carleton Co. Ontario. He died on 20 Feb 1893 in Ottawa Ontario[11].

iii. Samuel James Peer was born on 12 Jun 1857 in Brockville, Ontario. He died on 01 Jan 1915 in Toronto, York Co. Ontario[12].

iv. Oliver Peer was born about 1859 in Kitley Ontario. He married Lydia Ann Peer on 16 Aug 1882 in Leeds, Ontario.

4.**Stephen B. Peer**-2 (Peter-1) was born about 1824 in Canada. He died in 1888[4]. **Rosanna Tryon** was born about 1824 in Canada. She died in 1897 in Saginaw Michigan[4]. Stephen B. Peer and Rosanna Tryon were married on 01 Oct 1845 in Johnstown District Ontario[3].They had the following children:

i. John Peer was born about 1846 in Ontario.

ii. Stephen S. Peer was born in Oct 1847 in Canada. He married Mary Howard on 21 Nov 1880 in Shelby Co. Ohio. He died in 1905 in Sidney, Ohio.

iii. Joseph O. Peer was born about 1850 in Ontario.

iv. Henry Peer was born about 1854 in Ontario.

v. Jane Peer was born about 1855 in Ontario.

vi. Charles Morton or N. Peer was born about 21 Aug 1857 in Ontario. He married Carrie Kirkland on 09 Jun 1897 in Leeds & Grenville Co. Ontario. He died on 28 May 1921 in Bastard & Burgess Twp, Leeds Co. Ontario[13].

vii. Lewis M. Peer was born about 1860 in Canada. He died after 1891 in Saginaw Michigan.

viii. Lydia Ann Peer was born on 15 Feb 1862 in Bastard Tp Ontario. She married Oliver Peer on 16 Aug 1882 in Leeds, Ontario. She died on 05 Oct 1919 in Saginaw Michigan[14].

ix. Peter E. Peer was born about 1865 in Leamington, Ontario. He married Ada May Davis on 09 Sep 1897 in Ridgetown, Kent Co. Ontario[15].

x. Wallace Peer was born about 1870 in Canada.

5. **Mary Peer**-2 (Peter-1) was born about 1829 in Yonge Tp Ontario. She died after 1861. **Joseph Ducolon** son of Adam Ducolon and Mary was born about 1829 in Addison Ontario. He died after 1861. Joseph Ducolon and Mary Peer married.They had the following children:

i. Adam Ducolon was born in May 1853 in Addison, Elizabethtown Ontario. He married Mary Ann Henderson on 15 Jan 1878 in Leeds Co. Ontario. He died on 04 Jan 1918 in Athens Village, Leeds Co. Ontario[16].

ii. Peter Ducolon was born on 14 Apr 1855 in Addison, Elizabethtown Ontario. He married Alice Floy Ireland on 21 Feb 1900 in Leeds Co. Ontario. He died on 16 Jan 1928 in Leeds Co. Ontario[17].

iii. Mary Lucinda Ducolon was born about 15 Aug 1858 in Addison, Yonge Tp Ontario. She married George Henry Mott on 13 Aug 1878 in Leeds Co. Ontario. She died on 12 Mar 1921 in Leeds Co. Ontario[18].

iv. Lucinda Ducolon was born on 17 Jul 1861 in Elizabethtown Ontario. She married George Wesley Evans on 01 Jan 1879 in Leeds Co. Ontario. She died after 1911.

George Seeley. George Seeley and Mary Peer were married after 1860.They had no children.

6. **Hannah Peer**-2 (Peter-1) was born on 18 Mar 1833 in Addison, Elizabethtown-Kitley Tp, Leeds Co. Ontario[4]. She died on 07 Jun 1908 in Leeds Co. Ontario[5]. **Benjamin Scott** son of George Scott and Lucy Peterson was born on 09 Mar 1832 in Elizabethtown, Leeds Co. Ontario[4]. He died on 07 Oct 1915 in Leeds Co. Ontario[19]. Benjamin Scott and Hannah Peer were married between 1851-1854 in Ontario.They had the following children:

i. Alpheus Scott was born about 1854 in Ontario.

ii. Mary Scott was born about 1859 in Ontario.

iii. Joseph Scott was born about 1864 in Ontario.

iv. Emma Scott was born on 10 Oct 1873 in Ontario.

v. George W. Scott was born about 1875 in Elizabethtown Ontario. He married Pearl Hewitt on 02 Feb 1898 in Leeds Co. Ontario.

vi. Fleming Laurence was born on 02 Oct 1882 in Scotland.

vii. Alfred Scott.

7. **Britann (Ann) Peer**-2 (Peter-1) was born before 1828. **William Hanna**. William Hanna and Britann (Ann) Peer married.They had the following children:

i. Sara Hanna was born about 1848. She died on 30 Apr 1931 in Elizabethtown, Leeds Co. Ontario.

ii. William James Hanna was born on 27 Sep 1851 in Elizabethtown, Leeds Co. Ontario. He died on 29 Aug 1927 in Leeds Co. Ontario.

iii. Stephen Hanna was born about 1857 in Elizabethtown, Leeds Co. Ontario. He married Charlotte Driver on 29 Sep 1878 in Leeds Co. Ontario.

Peter Peer & Mary Graham Sources

1. Death Certificate, Reuben Peer living 10th Concession Elizabethtown, Leeds Co , farmer, widower, born Ontario, died of LaGrippe & pneumonia, 70 years old.
2. Death Certificate, Oliver Peer, age 83, born Elizabethtown, living Athens (Village) died of old age and general disability, gentleman, widower. T. G Sla----? made the return.
3. Johnstown District Marriage Register 1787-1850, 1845 Oct. 1 Stephen PAR (PEER), gentleman, to Rosannah Trion, lady, both of Yonge, by banns. Wit: Reuben Par (Peer),

gentleman, Samuel Wiltse, gentleman. Marriages performed by Rev. Cyrus R. Allison, Wesleyan Methodist/Methodist Episcopal Church.

4. John Charlton email February 2007.

5. Death Certificate.

6. Details: Name: Mina Cooper Birth Place: Elizabethtown Age: 19 Father Name: Henry Cooper Mother Name: Kate Cooper Estimated birth year: abt 1880 Spouse Name: William J Peer Spouse's Age: 35 Spouse Birth Place: Elizabethtown Spouse Father Name: Reuben Peer Spouse Mother Name : Margaret Peer Marriage Date: 7 Jun 1899 Marriage Place: Grenville Marriage County: Grenville Family History Library Microfilm: MS932_98 Source: Indexed by: Ancestry.com . Abbreviated Footnote: (null).

7. Death Certificate, William James Peer, age 40, living 10th concession, married, born Elizabethtown, suicide by hanging, no physician in attendance.

8. Details: Name: Clarissa Malvina Peer Date of Birth: 2 Sep 1873 Gender: Female Birth County: Leeds and Grenville Father's name: Reuben Peer, farmer in Elizabethtown Mother's name: Margret Chio [sic. This is probably the phonetic rendering of her name KEOGH] Roll Number: MS929_14 . Abbreviated Footnote: (null).

9. Marriage Certificate (Location: Mills Memorial Library, McMaster University, Hamilton Ontario;).

10. England Death Certificate, Sarah Jane Peer died Sept 29, 1901 age 65 living Lot 11, Conc 8, farmer's wife. married, born Ireland. heart Failure. Presbyterian. Informant SJ Peer.

11. Julie (Peer) Morphy Email 2002, died of consumption.

12. Ontario, Canada Deaths, 1869-1932 York 1915, Peer, Samuel J. 58 years old, died Jan. 1 1915 Toronto York Co. Born Brookville Ontario, father's name Oliver, mother's name not given. Died 27 Marmaduke St, of arterio sclerosis, iron moulder, married. Informant E M Peer, 27 Marmaduke.

13. Death Certificate, Charles Pier [sic] 64 years 9 months 7 days, died in Phillipsville, Irish origin, born in Bastard in 1857. Father Stephen Pier or Peer born July 11, 1821 in Bastard. Mother unknown born Bastard. His wife "Mrs. Pier" of Phillipsville was informant. Buried South Crosby died of pleurisy and tuberculosis.

14. Michigan Death Records 1897-1920.

15. Details: 007607-97 (Kent Co.) Peter E. PEER, driller, Leamington, Ridgetown, s/o Stephen & Rosanah, married Ada May DAVIS, 21, Michigan, Ridgetown, d/o John & Mary, witn: Emily BURDETTE & Margaret BOTTOM, both of Ridgetown, on 9 September 1897, at Ridgetown. Abbreviated Footnote: (null).

16. Death Certificate, Cheesemaker, married. Father Joseph Ducolon, Mother Mary Pier. Died of Bright's Disease. Mrs. Mary Ducolon was informant.

17. Death Certificate, married, born Apr 14, 1855 died age 73 years 9 mos 12 days. born Addison Ontario. Merchant of Second Hand goods. Father Joseph Ducolon Mother Mary Peer both born Elizabethtown. Mrs. Peter Ducolon, 9 Perth St, wife, was informant. Burial in Athens Ontario. Died of Carcinoma of prostate gland.

18. Death Certificate, Mary L. Mott, widow. Father Joseph Ducolon born Addison, Mother Mary Peer, born Yonge Tp. 63 years old, born Addison on Aug. 15th. Living 42 George St. Brockville. Informant Peter Ducolon, brother. Died of pulmonary tuberculosis.

19. Death Certificate, Benjamin Scott, living Athens, Leeds Co. Father George Scott. Informant Alfred Scott of Athens. 83 years 7 months old. Retired farmer, widower. Born Elizabethtown Tp Ontario. Cause of death - Metral Reg.

Other Ontario Peer Families: Richard Peer & Elizabeth Shouldice

This is an Irish Peer family who settled first in Quebec and then in the Ottawa area of Ontario. There does not appear to be any connection to our Peer family.

Richard Peer was born between 1807-1817 possibly in Ireland. He died between 1857-1871. He married Elizabeth Shouldice on 29 Sep 1837 in Bytown, Bathurst Ontario[1], daughter of James Shouldice and Jane Boyd. She was born on 03 Sep 1821 in Ireland or Bell's Corners, Ottawa, Carleton, Ontario. She died after 1871.

Children of Richard Peer and Elizabeth Shouldice are:

2. i. Richard Peer, B: 04 May 1840 in Masham, Gatineau, Quebec, D: 15 Aug 1891 in Duluth, Minnesota, M: Rebecca Shouldice, 09 Apr 1862 in Wakefield, Quebec.

ii. Jane Peer, B: 1842 in Quebec.

3. iii. James Peer, B: 1844 in Masham, Gatineau, Quebec, D: 20 Jul 1899 in Eastnor Tp, Bruce Co. Ontario[2], M: Elizabeth Shouldice, 08 Apr 1868 in Aylwin Quebec.

iv. Sarah Peer, B: 1846 in Ottawa County, Masham Quebec, D: 02 Jun 1919 in Eastnor, Bruce Co. Ontario[3].

v. John Peer, B: Abt. 1851 in Quebec.

4. vi. Margaret Peer, B: 27 Mar 1852 in Masham, Gatineau, Quebec, D: 30 Jan 1937 in Eastnor, Bruce County, Ontario, M: James Shouldice, 10 May 1871 in Aylwin, Quebec.

vii. Joseph Peer, B: Abt. 1857 in Quebec, M: Margaret Sang, 16 Oct 1883 in Bruce Co. Ontario.

Generation 2

2. **Richard Peer**-2(Richard-1) was born on 04 May 1840 in Masham, Gatineau, Quebec. He died on 15 Aug 1891 in Duluth, Minnesota. He married Rebecca Shouldice on 09 Apr 1862 in Wakefield, Quebec, daughter of Nicholas Shouldice and Ester Margaret Nesbitt. She was born on 07 Aug 1843 in Masham, Gatineau, Quebec. She died on 29 Apr 1907 in Duluth, Minnesota. Children of Richard Peer and Rebecca Shouldice are:

i. Margaret Jane Peer, B: 05 Feb 1863 in Quebec or Ottawa Ontario, D: 16 Oct 1934 in Minnedosa, Manitoba[4], M: Richard Delmage, 11 Jan 1887 in Bruce Co. Ontario.

ii. Nicholas Peer, B: 14 Nov 1865 in Quebec.

iii. Mary Agnes Peer, B: 25 Jun 1874.

iv. Elizabeth Peer, B: Abt. 1879 in Ontario.

v. Abigail Peer, B: 24 Sep 1879, D: 22 Feb 1942[4].

vi. Roseanna Peer, B: 10 Feb 1881 in Elderslie, Bruce Co. Ontario[5], D: 25 Mar 1889 in Bruce Co. Ontario[6].

3. **James Peer**-2(Richard-1) was born in 1844 in Masham, Gatineau, Quebec. He died on 20 Jul 1899 in Eastnor Tp, Bruce Co. Ontario[2]. He married Elizabeth Shouldice on 08 Apr 1868 in Aylwin Quebec, daughter of Nicholas Shouldice and Ester Margaret Nesbitt. She was born on 17 Jun 1845 in Masham, Gatineau, Quebec. She died in 1902 in Eastnor Tp, Bruce Co. Ontario. Children of James Peer and Elizabeth Shouldice are:

i. Sarah Alice (Alice) Peer, B: 25 Jan 1869 in Elora Ontario or Quebec, D: 23 Apr 1912 in Bruce Co. Ontario[7], M: Richard Boyle, 08 Jun 1887 in Eastnor, Bruce Co. Ontario[8].

ii. Ann Margaret Peer, B: 15 Jun 1871 in Quebec, D: 16 Aug 1911 in Lion's Head, Eastnor Tp, Bruce Co. Ontario[9], M: Thomas Pettigrew, 26 Sep 1900 in Bruce Co. Ontario.

iii. Nicholas Harvey Peer, B: 13 Mar 1874 in Quebec or Ontario, D: Aft. 04 Apr 1930.

iv. James Horace (Horace) Peer, B: 25 Aug 1875 in Quebec or Ontario, D: 04 Apr 1930 in Wiarton, Bruce County Ontario[10], M: Mary Tyndall, 30 Apr 1919 in Bruce Co. Ontario.

v. Eliza Rebecca Peer, B: Abt. 1880 in Sullivan Tp, (Quebec?), D: 19 Dec 1921 in Lion's Head, Bruce Co. Ontario[11], M: Samuel Henry Hayes, 22 Dec 1915 in Bruce Co. Ontario.

4. **Margaret Peer**-2(Richard-1) was born on 27 Mar 1852 in Masham, Gatineau, Quebec. She died on 30 Jan 1937 in Eastnor, Bruce County, Ontario. She married James Shouldice on 10 May 1871 in Aylwin, Quebec, son of Nicholas Shouldice and Ester Margaret Nesbitt. He was born on 17 Oct 1848 in Masham, Gatineau, Quebec. He died on 16 Feb 1928 in Eastnor, Bruce Co. Ontario. Children of Margaret Peer and James Shouldice are:

i. Richard Hiram Shouldice, B: Abt. 1875 in Quebec.

ii. Rugless Shouldice, B: Abt. 1877 in Eastnor Tp Bruce Co. Ontario, D: 1946.

iii. Emma Shouldice, B: Abt. 13 Dec 1879, D: 24 Aug 1898.

Richard Peer & Elizabeth Shouldice Sources

1. Ontario Marriages 1801-1930, Wakefield, Lower Canada. Witnesses Joseph Shouldice, William . Turney. Married by Presbyterian Minister of Bytown (Ottawa) Ontario.
2, Death Certificate, born Quebec, died of acute gastro enteritis had for 2 days. R. Boyle was the informant [his son in law] Living Conc 1W, Lot 12 Eastnor Tp Bruce Co.
3. Death Certificate, Sarah Peer, single. Age 74. Informant James Shouldice. Living Lot 15, Cocn 1, Eastnor Tp. Died of spinal sclorosis had for 3 years. Parents Richard Peer and Elizabeth Shouldice.
4. Eric Johannsen, http://familytreemaker.genealogy.com/users/j/o/h/Jon-E-Johannsen/BOOK- 0001/0017-0005.html.
5. Birth Registration, 002139 # 9 1845402. Rosana, d/o Richard Peer, farmer and Rebecca Shouldice of Elderslie, Bruce Co. Ontario.
6. Death Certificate.
7. Death Certificate, Sarah Alice Peer, died 23 Apr. 1912, age 43 years 2 months 29 days. born Quebec. Living Lot 43, Cocn 6, Lindsay, Bruce Co. Housewife. Parents James Peer, Elizabeth Shouldice both born Ottawa. Richard Boyle of Dyer's Bay was informant [her husband] No cause of death recorded.
8. Details: #001929-87 (Bruce Co): Richard BOYLE, 28, farmer, Peel twp., Eastnor, s/o Thomas & Elizabeth, married Alice PEER, 17, Elora, Eastnor, d/o James & Elizabeth, witn: Thomas BOYLE Jr. & Maggie PEER, both of Eastnor, 8 June 1887 at lot 12, con 1 west, Eastnor. Abbreviated Footnote: (null).
9. Death Certificate, Margaret Ann Pettigrew, born June 15, 1871 Quebec. Died in Lion's Head. Married. Parents James Peer, Elizabeth Shouldice both born Quebec. Informant Thomas Pettigrew of Lion's Head. Cause of death - insanity. Suicide, hanged herself. age 40 years 2 months 1 day.
10. Death Certificate, Informant Nicholas Harvey Peer of Lion's Head, brother. Father James Peer born Canada, mother Elizabeth Shouldice born Canada. Birthdate Oct. 4 1876. married. Living Wiarton Ontario.
11. Death Certificate, Eliza Rebecca Hayes, age 42 years 1 month 30 days. parents James Peer, Elizabeth both born Ireland [sic]. Born Sullivan Township, Oct 20, 1879. Informant husband H. E. Hayes, Lion's Head. Buried Eastnor Cemetery. Cause of death Albuminum Albucinumia. Confinement followed by convulsions, 1 hour

Other Ontario Peer Families: Andrew Peer & Helena Williamson

Andrew Peer is found in the Hamilton area of Ontario but as tempting as it might be to include him with our Peer family, his origins are Irish. He and his wife were both born in Ireland.

Andrew Peer was born about 1810 in Dublin Ireland. He married Helena W. Williamson.She was born about 1803 in Dublin Ireland. She died on 19 Feb 1868 in Hamilton, Wentworth Co. Ontario[1]. Children of Andrew Peer and Helena W. Williamson are:

3. i. Amelia Peer, B: 27 Oct 1844 in Toronto, Ontario, D: 31 Oct 1917 in Detroit, Wayne Co. Michigan[2], M: Joseph Carson, 19 Jan 1881 in Hamilton, Wentworth Co Ontario[3].

2. ii. Susan Peer, B: 04 Jul 1853 in Ontario, D: 18 Aug 1919 in Detroit, Wayne Co. Michigan[4].

Generation 2

2. **Susan Peer**-2(Andrew-1) was born on 04 Jul 1853 in Ontario. She died on 18 Aug 1919 in Detroit, Wayne Co. Michigan[4]. She married Richard Bransby Cronin.He was born about 1850 in England. Children of Susan Peer and Richard Bransby Cronin are:

i. Andrew Lewis Cronin, B: 01 Aug 1871 in Hamilton, Wentworth Co. Ontario.

ii. Amelia Cronin, B: 17 Aug 1873 in Lincoln Co. Ontario.

iii. Agnes Eveline Ross Cronin, B: 19 Jul 1875 in Hamilton, Wentworth Co. Ontario.

iv. Frederick Charles Miller Cronin, B: 14 May 1877 in Hamilton, Wentworth Co. Ontario.

v. Helena Cronin, B: 14 Sep 1879 in Hamilton, Wentworth Co. Ontario.

vi. Alenia Cronin, B: Abt. 1880 in Ontario.

vii. Arthur Dennis Cronin, B: 03 May 1882 in Hamilton, Wentworth Co. Ontario.

3. **Amelia Peer**-2(Andrew-1) was born on 27 Oct 1844 in Toronto, Ontario. She died on 31 Oct 1917 in Detroit, Wayne Co. Michigan[2]. She married Joseph Carson on 19 Jan 1881 in Hamilton, Wentworth Co Ontario[3], son of James Carson and Mary W..

He was born about 1848 in East Flamboro Ontario. He died before Oct 1917. Child of Amelia Peer and Joseph Carson is:

i. Mary Helena Cathleen Carson, B: 03 May 1885 in Wentworth Co. Ontario.

Andrew Peer & Helena Williamson Sources

1. The Hamilton Evening Times, Wednesday, February 19, 1868 P 3. Died in this city on the 19th inst.[same month] Helen, the beloved wife of Mr. Andrew Peer, age 65 years.
2. Michigan Death Records 1897-1920, Father Andrew Peer born Ireland, mother Helena Williamson no birth location. Widowed.
3. Ontario Archives, Marriage Registration, 1869512 Reg #12616. Joseph Carson, 33 living E. Flamboro, farmer, b. E. Flamboro to James & Mary W. Carson, Roman Catholic, m Amelia Peer, 27, living Hamilton born Toronto to Andrew & Helena W. Peer, Roman Catholic. Wit Patrick Carson, Susan M. Mahoney, Hamilton.
4. Michigan Death Records 1897-1920, Father Andrew Peer born Dublin Ireland. Mother Helena Williamson born Dublin Ireland.

Other Ontario Peer Families: Andrew Peer & Elizabeth

According to the 1901 census Andrew Peer did not arrive in Ontario until 1843 and he was born in Scotland. He does not connect to our Peer family.

Andrew Peer was born on 09 May 1830 in Scotland. He married Elizabeth.She was born on 25 Aug 1835 in Scotland. Children of Andrew Peer and Elizabeth are:

i. Euphemia Peer, B: 24 May 1861 in Ontario.

ii. Elizabeth Peer, B: 01 Mar 1871 in Ontario.

iii. Russell Peer, B: 22 Apr 1882 in Ontario.

DNA Research

So where does the diligent genealogist go from here? How do we find evidence for our Jacob Peer's heritage and birth? I suggest we must focus on DNA research.

DNA research is a fairly new avenue of genealogical research and it is gaining popularity among serious researchers. I personally have been tested with three companies and have connected with others who share genomes with me. This "cousin connection" allows individuals to share their family trees, discuss their common ancestor(s) and help each other to take another step backwards on their ancestor tree. It also allows individuals to verify or disprove their connection to locations and a specific branch of a surname.

In the case of our Peer family what we need is to test as many males who still have the Peer surname. With the Y-DNA test that only men can have done, we would be able to determine (if enough males have the test done) whether or not we are connected through DNA to the Pier line in New York, or a Peer line in Germany or any number of other locations and branches.

Women have two X-Chromosomes while while men have one X-Chromosome and one Y-Chromosome. Every individual receives one Chromosome from the mother and one from the father. Thus the Y chromosone is passed from father to son which allows male ancestry to be tracked back through generations of unbroken males.

Testing female mitochondrial DNA will not work for us in this case as that MtDNA is passed from mother to daughter unbroken going back through the family tree. So for example my MtDNA is from my mother and hers from her mother (my maternal grandmother) and my maternal grandmother's from her mother and so on.

The optimum scenario is to test male Peer relatives who are confirmed as descending from Jacob and Anna, and also test Peer males who are confirmed as descending from the New York Pier line descending from the brothers Arent and Jan Teunissen. Any other Peer branches with Peer males willing to test would help. The more Peer males who have their DNA tested, the better.

Both men and women can have an Autosomal DNA test done but the Y-DNA test is more helpful to us in this case. My recommendation is that any male Peer individuals willing to get their Y-DNA test done, have a minimum of 37 markers tested. The more markers, the better. The only company offering the Y-DNA test is FamilyTreeDNA (FTNDA). If you join the Peer Surname Group first, you can order your kit at a discounted price. To find this group go to https://www.familytreedna.com and choose letter "P" in the Y-DNA SURNAME PROJECTS chart.

Endnotes

[1] Crown Patents Beverley Tp. Conc. 8 Lot 32 South 1/2, 100 acres July 5, 1853. Andrew Peer, from Ireland 1852

[2] See 1871 and 1881 Census for Hamilton, Wentworth County Ontario

[3] Sussex County was formed in 1753 from part of Morris County, which was formed in 1738 from part of Hunterdon County, which was formed in 1714 from part of Burlington County, which was formed in 1694 as an orginal county.   Frankford Tp. was split from the northern half of Newton Tp.

[4] Revolutionary Census of New Jersey: an Index Based on Rateables, of the Inhabitants of New Jersey during the period of The American Revolution" by Kenn Stryker-Rodda

[5] History of Sussex Co. by Snell., Frankford Tp. Sussex Co. Marriages by Squire Franklin Price.

[6] *Revolutionary Census of New Jersey: an Index Based on Rateables, of the Inhabitants of New Jersey during the period of The American Revolution* by Kenn Stryker-Rodda. Hunterdon House. Lambertville NJ. 1986 p. 106

[7] *Revolutionary Census of New Jersey: an Index Based on Rateables, of the Inhabitants of New Jersey during the period of The American Revolution* by Kenn Stryker-Rodda. Hunterdon House. Lambertville NJ. 1986 P 108

[8] Papakating Creek flows into the Wallkill River just below the borough of Sussex. Its origin is near Beemerville which is on the border of Wantage and Franford Township. We know from land records that Jacob's son Levi owned land "at the head of" this Creek, and he was also listed as "of Wantage". This provides us with a fairly precise location for the Peer family before 1800

[9] 1797, 13 July: John Peer of Ancaster petitioned for 200 acres of land stating he had been nine years in the Province and had a family, and had never received any certificate or order of Council for land. C-2489 Bundle 3/43

[10] Military "C" Records. FHL 1753825.

[11] U.S. Census Reconstructed Records, 1660-1820

[12] Petitions and Other Papers relating to Bridges, Canals, Dams, Ferries and Roads, 1765-1835 [New Jersey State Archives]; Call Number: Box 4, Folder 56; ; Page Number: 1; Family Number: 1.

[13] Statement by Nathaniel Pettit dated 10 July 1797

[14] Upper Canada Land Petitions C-2489 Bundle 3/70

[15] Loyalist Lineages of Canada 1783-1983 by Audrey F. Kirk, U.E. and Robert F. Kirk

[16] Upper Canada Land Book C 1st July, 1797 - 31st July, 1797 p. 81 July 14

[17] Upper Canada Land Petition dated 13 July 1797, stating he had been "in the Province 9 years" and had a family

[18] Statistics Canada. http://www.statcan.ca/english/freepub/98-187-XIE/upcan.htm

[19] Sussex County Deeds: Page 35 [Original Book] courtesy of Chris Brooks

[20] C-2489 Bundle 3/70

[21] Sussex County Deeds: Page 253 [Original Book] courtesy of Chris Brooks

[22] FHL 1753825

[23] C-2489 V. 400 P 2/46

[24] C-2489 Bundle 3/43

[25] C 101

[26] Family information and Seth Hastings Grant Collection at New England Historic Genealogical Society and Library in Boston Courtesy of Valarie Albert

[27] Upper Canada Land Petitions S12/325 Vol 460A C-2813 LDS 1630749. Courtesy of Valarie Albert

[28] See Chapter on Philip Peer and reference to John Binkley

[29] Courtesy of Valarie Albert

[30] C-1076. p. 76 ED 3

[31] Second River RDC, Belleville, Essex Co. NJ Sponsors Reynier Van Giesen; Mettje Vreelant. Parents Johannes Pier, Susanna Rattan

www.ingramcontent.com/pod-product-compliance
Lightning Source LLC
Chambersburg PA
CBHW060858270326
41935CB00003B/23